MUSICIANS INSTITUTE™

PRIVATE LESSONS

THE MUSICIAN'S GUIDE
RECORDING *Drums*

by Dallan Beck

ALSO BY DALLAN BECK:
The Musician's Guide to Recording Acoustic Gu
The Musician's Guide to Recording Vocals (book/CD)
Home Recording Basics (video)

ISBN 0-634-05714-6

HAL•LEONARD® CORPORATION

7777 W. BLUEMOUND RD. P.O. BOX 13819 MILWAUKEE, WI 53213

Visit Hal Leonard Online at
www.halleonard.com

In Australia Contact:
Hal Leonard Australia Pty. Ltd.
22 Taunton Drive P.O. Box 5130
Cheltenham East, 3192 Victoria, Australia
Email: ausadmin@halleonard.com

Table of Audio Contents

Table of Contents

Introduction

Welcome to my third book in this Musicians Institute series. My first two books, *The Musician's Guide to Recording Acoustic Guitar* and *The Musician's Guide to Recording Vocals*, provided the beginning recordist with in-depth coverage on fundamental recording topics such as equalization, compression, gating, effects parameters, and definitions, as well as a run-down on microphone types (condenser and dynamic) and polar patterns; and this book will be no different. This book will also include graphic illustrations detailing the essential settings to use for signal processing and effects.

Because the focus of this book is not only on live drum recording, but on getting a professional sound, I'm going to begin with the most basic of setups and work up to larger and more complex ones. Some of you already have a variety of microphones, a great drum kit, a console, processors, and a great drum room to record in. However, I believe that most of you have instead some type of home-based or "project" studio setup and will be recording with a fixed number of microphones in a drum room that was not designed or built by a professional. Regardless of which setup you have, I suggest you read this book from the beginning to the end. The information in each section is neither "only basic" nor "only advanced," but always a mixture of both. Sometimes, just a single piece of information separates a good drum sound from a great drum sound; so don't skip the details. Consider this a workbook, to be gone through from beginning to end. So have fun and enjoy the information.

Before You Begin

In order to get the most out of the information I've provided here, you'll need to understand how to read and interpret the figures that illustrate the various instructions in this book. You will also need to have the minimum equipment requirements that I've outlined below.

Equipment Basics

In order to implement the recording techniques and reproduce the results described in this book, you will need the following items:

- Microphones (between two to fifteen)
- Drum kit and drummer
- Drum room (in which to record the drums)
- Recording gear:
    - XLR cables and microphone stands
    - Mixer with mic preamps
    - Basic signal processors
    - Multitrack (computer or stand-alone unit)
- Reference CDs

Microphones

You can use as few as two microphones to record drums. This means, of course, that you will have fewer options for modifying the drums' sounds; but if you use some of techniques that I've provided in this book, you can still record professional-sounding drums. The largest mic setup I will illustrate in this book will use fifteen microphones simultaneously. Even though I don't expect that everyone will have that big of a setup, I want to show you some options that you may use if you have a chance to record in a professional recording studio.

I'm going to strongly suggest that, if you only have two microphones, they be *condenser* microphones. Once you get into the use of four or more microphones, I will suggest any additional types to use. If you currently have two *dynamic* microphones, then so be it. Your sounds will be different than mine, but the techniques are still usable. (As a guideline, I will reference the brands and models of microphones that I use; so if you have the same microphones, you can match accordingly.)

If you're unfamiliar with the different types of microphones, their characteristics, and polar patterns, refer to chapter 2.

Drum Kit and Drummer

I may be stating the obvious for some of you, but I would be remiss if I did not mention that one of the biggest factors to getting professional drums sounds depends on both the quality of the drum kit and the proficiency of the drummer.

Before you begin recording, ask your drummer to acquire new drumheads. Old drumheads sound dull and lifeless, and have trouble staying in tune. Speaking of which: also ask your drummer to meticulously tune the drumheads in order to remove all of the unnecessary pitch waves that occur from an unbalanced drumhead.

Although I could write entire chapters on the importance of drum tuning and snare/kick dampening (and I have included sections on each), the ins and outs of these responsibilities are best left to a skilled and capable drummer. As a recordist, it is important to understand drum mechanics, but drummers are usually experts in their own right for these kinds of things. I prefer to just point out a few sonic problems and let the drummer adjust the kit accordingly. Because I usually place microphones within close proximity to the drums, I can hear the sounds that will be recorded more accurately than the drummer in an open room can. That's why I always let the drummer listen to the sounds I'm hearing and ask him or her to make adjustments—anything from fixing squeaky pedals, loosening drum heads for more emphasis and low-end, fine-tuning the tom heads, or dampening the kick and snare, etc.

When recording the drum sounds for this book, we used an OCP custom drum kit and a variety of snares and cymbals. All of the drums were in excellent shape and had been cared for by the drummer. I also chose an amazing drummer, Jeff Bowders. I met him at a session a few years ago and never forgot what a solid player he was. When he hits the drums, he does so with conviction. This is the ultimate secret to getting good drum sounds: find an exceptional drummer—one who plays with groove and feel, has solid timing, and has excellent control over his or her dynamics. Most of the problems that I have encountered when recording drums were due to the drummer's inconsistent groove or weak technique and/or a poor quality drum kit.

Drum Room

I am again going to assume that you are recording your drums in some sort of a "project" studio environment—a bedroom, garage, rehearsal facility, etc. In that case, the main objective is to remove as much reflecting sound waves as possible. I will mention this again in chapter 5, when we talk about recording with two room microphones, but please start to prepare now. What we want to do is baffle or block as many of the reflections off the walls and ceilings as possible. This can be done with padding, foam, carpeting, or professional products. Our aim is to eliminate all reflections from the sound created when you clap your hands in the middle of the room. TRACK 01 is an example of the reflections that occur from a clap in the middle of a room. Compare that to TRACK 02, which features a clap recorded in a room with the same dimensions, but with walls and ceilings padded with soundboard and foam padding, and a rug on the floor. Notice the difference? I'm not saying that one sound was necessarily better than the other; but live reflections are problematic when recording. And if the reflected sound is what I want, I would much rather control it by adding effects later that will simulate these same sounds.

Of course, if you are recording in a professional room, there's no need to pad or otherwise modify it. I use the dampening only in rooms prone toward unwanted or unintended reflections.

Recording Gear (Cables, Mic Stands, Mixer, Preamp, Processors, and Multitrack)

Obviously, you will need a microphone cable for every mic you plan to use, as well as an available input for each of them. Most microphones use XLR (3-pin) cables, so you'll need a mixer that accepts this type of plug-in. Some multitracks have built-in mixers with two to eight XLR inputs that connect to internal *mic preamps*—preamps that boost the converted sound to the appropriate level for recording. Each of your microphones will need to be connected to a mic preamp. But unlike *line preamps*, which only boost up to about 20 decibels (dB), mic preamps boost up to 70 or 80 dB. An average mic preamp setting is about 30 dB (some sounds will need as little as 10 dB; others will need as much as 50 or 60 db).

Because your recording capabilities will be limited by such things as: (1) the number of tracks you can record on simultaneously, (2) the number of microphone inputs you can use simultaneously, and/or (3) the number of microphones you have available, I am going to start with a simple two-microphone setup. Almost any recording setup, from a cassette 4-track to a computer rig, should be able to accommodate this configuration. However, when we address the issue of adding more microphones, you'll need to overcome all three of the above limitations in order to replicate the setups I discuss. The one exception will be when "submixing" or combining tracks. This technique is done when you have a sufficient number of microphones and inputs, but are running out of tracks to record on. Instead of recording each one on a separate track, you will end up blending the sounds on that track. I will do this when I use more than one microphone for an individual drum sound, like kick or snare.

The signal processors that I will use to enhance or alter the original drum sounds include parametric equalizer, compressor, gate, and reverb. I have chosen plug-in processors for the purpose of this book, so that I can incorporate illustrations on what is discussed (and also because they are very flexible and affordable).

Reference CDs

It's important that you select some drum sounds from existing CDs or other recordings against which you can compare your own practice recordings. When listening to these "reference CDs," pay close attention to the level balances of each drum sound in relation to the other drums. You should also listen for: the panning of each instrument, and where within the stereo field you hear each one; the quality or tone of each instrument in relation to the brightness or fatness, attack or punch of each sound; and effects (like reverb). Your goal will be to replicate these drum sounds and effects on your own recording.

However, keep in mind that, when it comes to judging the *quality* of your sound compared to that on the reference CD, there are too many variables for such an assessment to be effective. For example, every speaker system is different, as is every room that houses those speakers—and these differences change the way sound is actually captured on a recording. But the reference CD can help you to minimize these discrepancies. So, go through your CD collection or go to the store and find a drum sound that you feel is appropriate for the song(s) you are recording. After asking a few drummers which CDs featured drums sounds that they admired, I went and picked up about half a dozen CDs specifically for this book. After all, unless the drummer is nearly deaf from not wearing ear plugs, who else could I trust to really listen and admire drum sounds?

Microphones

A microphone is a *transducer*—that is, something that converts one form of energy into another. In our case, sound waves are converted into electrical current.

Dynamic vs. Condenser

There are two types of microphones: dynamic and condenser. *Dynamic* mics are based on a magnetic principle and convert sound to electrical current. These mics do this through the use of a moving coil. In simplest terms, the louder the input signal, the more the coil moves, the more sound /electrical current is transferred through the mic. Because of this, dynamic mics are best for handling loud, transient sounds. They're also good for rejecting feedback (from monitors), which makes them great for live performance. Because they are self-powered, dynamic mics are ready to use simply by plugging them into a preamp—that is, the "mic level" input of your mixer or multitrack recorder, or a separate, stand-alone unit.

The second type of mic is the *condenser*, which works on an electrostatic principle to convert sound into current. It only takes a minimal amount of sound to move the charged particles inside a condenser mic; as a result, these mics are very sensitive and pick up subtleties, nuances, and tone exceptionally well. Some cannot handle heavy sound pressure levels (SPL); others can handle moderate to heavy SPL. ("Heavy SPL" being loud guitar amps and certain drums; in the case of vocals, you'll rarely find a vocalist who is too loud for the mic.) Condenser mics do an amazing job of recording every little nuance in a vocal; plus, they are available with various polar patterns, which pick up sounds from different directions or multiple sources.

Condensers are usually powered by an external source called *phantom power* (48 volts). This means that, unless your condenser mic uses an internal battery, it will draw power from whatever you plug it into—like a mixer or external preamp. (Though phantom power has become a standard new feature on most such units, you should check to be sure yours has it before you purchase a brand new condenser mic; otherwise, when you plug it in, it just won't work.) Condensers, by the way, can be solid-state, tube (a.k.a. "valve"), or a hybrid of both. (These terms refer to how the mic processes the input signal, which to a greater or lesser degree, will affect its sound—much like with a guitar amp.)

The examples throughout this book will indicate the type of mic being used (dynamic or condenser), illustrate the best placement configurations for capturing optimal sound quality, offer model recommendations, and explain why a particular model is the mic of choice.

Polar Patterns

What do you need your microphone to do? In other words, are you recording more than one drum or drum accessory at a time? Are you in a professional, acoustically tuned room, or in your basement, bedroom, or garage? These factors will impact your choice of microphone *polar pattern*—the range, or pattern, around a mic from which it picks up sound. Condenser mics offer different polar patterns, each with its own advantages and disadvantages, depending on your particular recording needs.

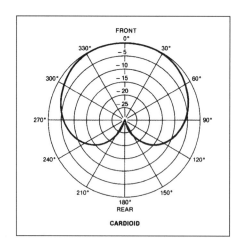

Cardioid

The most common polar pattern for dynamic and condenser mics is cardioid. Cardioid patterns respond to sound mainly from the front of the mic, less from the sides, and reject sound from the rear. This pattern is your best choice for individual miking techniques, and minimizing unwanted bleed from other sounds.

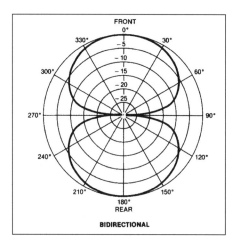

Bi-Directional

Also known as the figure-8 polar pattern, the bi-directional pattern captures sounds at the front and back of the mic, while rejecting sound from the sides. Bi-directional patterns can be used when sharing a single microphone in between 2 toms on a drum kit.

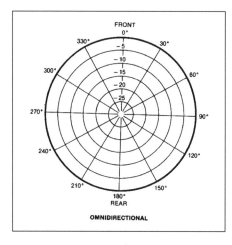

Omni-Directional

The omni-directional polar pattern (omni meaning all) picks up sound in a 360-degree range. This pattern is good for room microphones and possibly overheads, when you are willing to include the room reflections in the recording.

Not sure which pattern is right for the majority of your needs? Some condenser mics come with a switchable polar pattern. These mics however, will be your most expensive option.

Mic Pad

Many condenser mics have a built-in attenuation switch, commonly known as a *pad*. The pad reduces the amount of input signal so the microphone doesn't distort when recording loud sounds.

Although all of the drum sounds are loud, the pad becomes necessary only when the microphone is in close proximity to the instrument. A good example is the snare drum. It has such an explosive and cutting sound, that when using a condenser on it, I find that a pad is always necessary. Your alternatives to using a pad are: using a dynamic mic instead, miking up on angles that are off-axis, or pulling the microphone farther away from the instrument. I only use these other options if the condenser that I want to use does not have a pad.

Roll-Off, Cut-Off, and Proximity Effect

A *roll-off* is a filter built into the microphone. It generally removes sounds beneath a chosen frequency. The picture here shows both a roll-off and a cut-off. The *cut-off* is removing frequencies lower than 80 Hz, at a rate of 18 dB/octave; the roll-off is gradually removing frequencies starting just above 200 Hz, at a rate of 6 dB/octave.

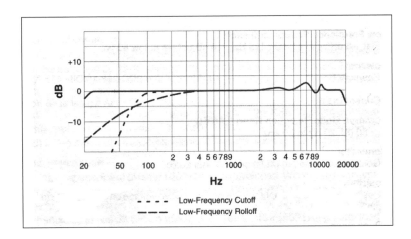

Roll-off and/or cut-off are used to reduce ultra-low and overall low-end frequencies caused by proximity effect movement. *Proximity effect* happens when a source is too close to the mic and exaggerates the amount of low-end present in the sound. A little low-end might be fine, but too much can muddy the sound. Movement of the mic or the mic stand can also generate low frequency noise, which some people refer to as "rumble."

Sound Processors

Before we get into the following chapters, each of which will cover to some extent the use of processors to manipulate and blend sounds, I want to provide a brief overview on how these processors—compression, EQ, editing, gating, and reverb—will affect the drum sounds we'll be recording.

Also, in order to discuss these processors as simply and visually as possible, I've incorporated photos and screen-shot images to illustrate how, via mic placement, equipment parameters, etc., I am able to achieve the results described. The following sections demonstrate how to read such graphic features for the compressor, EQ, limiter, and gate.

Compression

Compression is used to focus the sound, as well as alter it to be either punchier or softer, or more resonant (loose) or less resonant (tight). We speak of the compression settings in terms of the degree of *attack* and length of *release*:

Slower attack setting: the punchier the sound

Faster attack setting: the smoother or softer the sound

Shorter release time: the more resonant and bigger the sound

Longer release time: the tighter the sound

You can combine the attacks and releases to obtain the following results:

Slower attack/longer release: punchier/tighter

Faster attack/shorter release: smooth/resonant-big

Slower attack/shorter release: punchier/resonant-big

Faster attack/longer release: smooth/tighter

When using **compression**, you will also need to set the **ratio**, **threshold**, and **output** controls. Lower **ratios** require lower **thresholds**, but are less noticeable—like when you just want a little more punch or resonance. Higher ratios are more drastic and better suited for smoothing out sounds, rather than for adding punch. The **threshold** is to be set by ear, until the desired amount of compression has occurred. The **output** should be used to balance out any loss caused by compression.

How far compression can manipulate or alter your sound depends upon the quality of the dry recording and getting optimal mic placement.

Figure 1 is a screen shot of a compressor, for which I've separated and described the individual parameters—threshold, ratio, attack, release, attenuation, and gain/output.

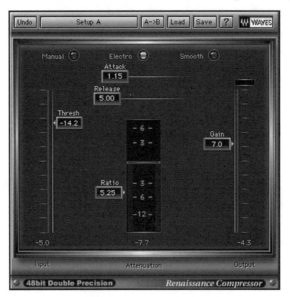

Fig. 1 – Compressor

Threshold

Measured in decibels (dB), the *threshold* setting is the point at which you determine what part of the sound gets compressed, and what part doesn't need it. The meter to the left shows the peak levels of the sound you are compressing, which you watch to determine where the peaks are. The number at the bottom of the meter (here –5.0 dB) shows you the highest peak to occur so far. Based on this peak reading, if I were to set the threshold higher than –5.0 dB ("higher" meaning closer to 0), no compression would occur, because none of the sounds are "loud" enough for the compression function to kick in. For compression to occur, I would have to set the threshold to at least –6.0 dB. However, at this setting, only 1.0 dB of sound would "qualify" for compression (the difference between the –6.0 dB setting and the –5.0 dB peak). In Figure 1, the threshold is set at –14.2 dB, meaning that 9.2 decibels "qualify" for compression (the difference between –14.2 dB setting and –5.0 dB peak). That doesn't mean, however, that I will have 9.2 dB of compression reduction; other parameters, discussed in the following sections, also influence how much of this sound will actually be compressed.

NOTE: I don't use math so much to decide my settings; I'm at a point where I've had enough experience and I just use my ears. But I do fully understand all possible parameters, so that if I'm not getting the desired result, I know which parameters need to be adjusted.

Ratio

The *ratio* parameter determines how much of the sound above the threshold actually gets compressed. The ratio shown on Figure 1 is 5.25 (or 5.25:1). This means that for every five decibels of sound above the threshold setting, one decibel will *not* be compressed (but four decibels will be). This translates to about an 80% ratio of sound that will be compressed vs. sound not compressed. Why not compress 100%? Because, in order for the compression to sound natural, some dynamics must remain. Therefore the ratio setting allows dynamic flexibility.

When the ratio becomes higher than 10:1 or above, we create a limiter. A *limiter* has the ability to remove the dynamics because it creates an invisible, inflexible level that cannot be breached. Again, depending on the other parameters (especially threshold and attack, which is discussed in the next section), the limiter can be used in many different ways for various sound results.

Attack

The *attack* setting is measured in milliseconds (ms). Figure 1 shows a 1.15 ms setting. This parameter determines how quickly the compressor will react to apply the ratio when the sound goes above the threshold. Lower settings reduce the amount of attack, or "punch," from the original sound, and higher settings allow the attack to get by the compressor, resulting in a punchier sound.

Release

The *release* is also measured in milliseconds. Figure 1 shows a 5 ms setting. This parameter sets how quickly the compressor stops applying the ratio when the sound has dropped below the threshold setting. If it turns off too soon, we will hear the compressor letting go of the sound, creating a rapid increase in volume that should instead, in most cases, be smooth and not heard. If, on the other hand, we set compressor release too long, the compressor would continue to reduce the volume of the track, even though it is no longer necessary (a common form of compressor abuse, for which they unfairly get a bad name.)

Attenuation

The *attenuation* is a read-out or resulting number, measured in decibels (dB), that tells you how much compression you have used—in other words, how much the peaks were brought down in volume. The attenuation in Figure 1 is 7.7 dB (the read-out on this type of plug-in does not show the average compression applied, but the peak, or highest amount used at any time). Some compressors have to be watched, as they fluctuate instead of retaining their peak settings. The attenuation reading is very important, because it indicates how to set the gain parameter (discussed below).

Gain/Output

The *gain*, also known as *output* or *make-up*, is measured in decibels (dB). The setting on Figure 1 is 7 dB, which indicates the amount of overall volume that has been added due to the amount of attenuation (or gain reduction) that has occurred. This gain setting should match the attenuation/dB reduction setting.

The output setting indicates how far away you are from peaking or distorting. Figure 1 shows a reading of –4.3 dB from distortion. This means that even though the gain should be set to match the attenuation level, I could add up to 4.3 dB more of gain and still not distort or *clip*. Likewise, if the output setting is too hot, I may have to decrease my gain below the attenuation, in order to avoid distorting.

Here is an example of the relation between attenuation and gain. If I have compressed a maximum of 7.7 dB, then I can increase or make-up the output by that same amount; doing so will *add* 7.7 dB of sound to all of the sounds that were not compressed, which makes all of the softer sounds much fuller. Also, because I *reduced* my peaking sounds by 7.7 dB, I am going to be bringing them right back to where they started. Do the math: (–7.7) + 7.7 = ? Zero. So, the peaks remain at the same level as before compression, but the added result is that the smaller, softer sounds are 7.7 dB louder without fear of distortion. This is the real magic of compression.

Equalization (EQ)

An *equalizer*, or EQ, is used to adjust the sound's *tone*—bass, middle, and treble response. The EQ alters the color of the sound, making it brighter, darker, warmer, harsher, more nasal, less nasal, fuller, thinner, etc. There are a host of adjectives that are used to describe the results of using EQ.

EQ settings are different for each instrument, but you can add and/or take away frequencies to get desired results. See the EQ settings for the individual drum components for frequency setting examples and how they affect each sound.

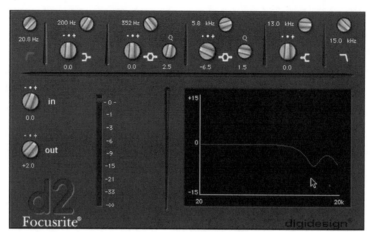

Fig. 2 – EQ

Figure 2 shows a parametric equalizer, which gives you control over the bandwidth and frequency choices (sound frequencies are described in hertz, Hz, or kilohertz, KHz. Hertz are the low and low-mid frequencies, while kilohertz are the upper-mid and high frequencies.

Fig. 3 – Hz knob   *Fig. 4 – KHz knob*

The *Hz* (hertz) knob of Figure 3, and the *KHz* (kilohertz) knob of Figure 4 determine the frequencies that you may wish to alter. Because the parametric EQ shown in Figure 2 has a total of six simultaneous frequency knobs, this is known as a 6-band parametric EQ.

Two of the knobs, however, act only as *filters*; they cannot boost frequencies—only reduce them. These knobs are located on the far ends at the upper left and right. They are set at 20.8 Hz and 15.0 KHz, respectively.

Symbols

It is also important to look closely at the symbols depicted on the EQ. The one on the right is turned "on," or *active*, while the one on the left is grayed out, or *inactive*. This means that the high-frequency filter (known as *low-pass*) is actually working, while the low-frequency filter (known as *high-pass*) is not turned on. Watch the symbols closely to see if the frequencies are active and working when trying to copy the settings in this book.

 The symbol of Figure 5 indicates that the frequency can be cut or boosted in equal amounts below the selected frequency.

Fig. 5

The symbol shown in Figure 6 indicates that the frequency can be cut or boosted in equal amounts above the selected frequency.

Fig. 6

Figure 7's *shelf* symbol indicates that the frequency can be cut only above the selected frequency. This means it is a *filter*.

Fig. 7

The shelf symbol of Figure 8 indicates that the frequency can be cut only below the selected frequency. This is also a filter.

Fig. 8

The *bell* symbol shown in Figure 9 indicates that the frequency selected will be affected most—either boosted or cut. However, frequencies higher and lower than the selected frequency will also be affected, but in lesser amounts the farther they are from the selected frequency. How wide a range of frequencies will be affected is determined by the Q *setting*.

Fig. 9

Figure 10's Q *setting* controls the bandwidth of the frequency selected. This setting is based on a mathematical formula, but is more easily understood by the following: the lower the setting (0.2–2.0), the more frequencies that are affected; the higher the setting (2.5+), the fewer frequencies that are affected, or the narrower the bandwidth in that given area. Q creates a bell-like umbrella that places the target frequency at the center. The farther you go—either higher or lower—the less effect the EQ has on the farther frequencies.

Fig. 10

Boost / Cut Knob

The *boost/cut* knob depicted in Figure 11 shows you how many decibels have been added (positive read-out) or removed (negative read-out) at a selected frequency.

Fig. 11

Input / Output Levels

The *input/output* knobs shown in Figure 12 control the amount of input gain and output gain for the EQ. When a signal is boosted heavily by EQ, the output could need to be reduced to compensate for the increase in frequencies.

Fig. 12

Conversely, like Figure 12 shows, the output may need to be increased if frequencies are being removed. When boosts and cuts are balanced, the output is normally left at 0 dB, or *unity gain*.

Meter

 The *meter*, as shown in Figure 13, gauges the amount of EQ output. Its readout will help you determine whether or not to reduce or increase your output level.

Fig. 13

If the level is too high, the peak indicator, at the top of the meter above the 0 marker, will light up.

Display

Figure 14 illustrates the *display*, which shows how the frequency, boost/cut, and Q knobs have affected the sound by indicating the bandwidth and any peaks clearly.

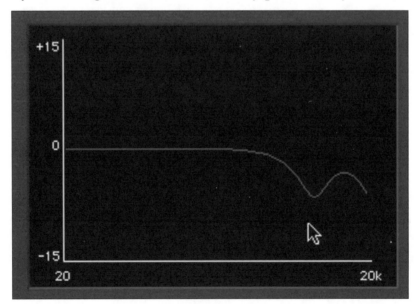

Fig. 14

Limiter

A *limiter* increases the volume or density of a track. It removes some of the peaks, or transients, that register as clips. The result is that extra headroom is gained, and the overall track becomes louder. Unlike compression, which is used for an audible difference, the limiter's effect is unnoticeable. I will use the limiter herein for two things: to discretely raise the volume of a track, and to remove the possibility of clipping.

The limiter, as shown in Figure 15, has four displays:

Fig. 15 – Limiter

Threshold

The lower the threshold becomes, the louder the track becomes. Depending on the average volume of the track, compression caused through limiting will become noticeable when the threshold is lowered too much.

Out Ceiling

This display sets the maximum output (peak) of the track. (I always play it a little safe and set it to –0.1 or –0.2.)

Release

The release is the same as the compressor. The higher the value of release, the more compression you'll get, but the result will be perceptible; if set too low, you'll hear the compressor turning on and off frequently.

Attenuation

Attenuation, or *atten* for short, means "change." This display represents the amount of decibels being limited. This is also a good indicator of whether or not you're using too much threshold. Too little threshold and the read-out will remain at 0 or 1 dB; too much will be noticeable at or above 7 dB, depending on the density and dynamics of the track.

Gate

I will use a *gate* for two reasons: 1) to clean up the track and remove unwanted noise, or "bleed" (from other sounds); and 2) to clean up and smooth out edits that create a clipped or abrupt ending.

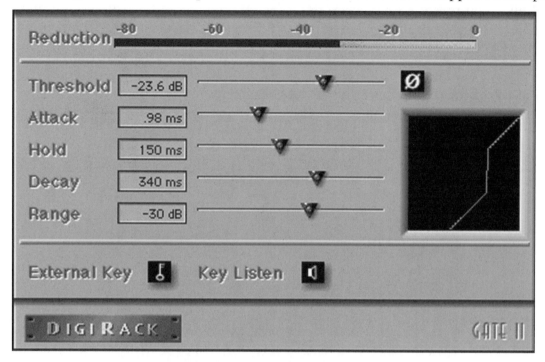

Fig. 16 – Gate with parameters

The gate, which is shown in Figure 16, has six parameters:

Reduction

This meter shows, in decibels, the value set at *range* (see #2). It also moves in real time with the track to show the "opening" and "closing" of the gate.

Range

The range is the amount of reduction in decibels. Only as much range as is needed to remove, or just reduce, the bleed from other track should be applied. When the range is set too low, the gate sounds very mechanical and takes away from the open sound of the track.

Threshold

This is the level at which the gate opens and closes. The objective is to set this level higher than that of any unwanted peaks, but lower than all desired sounds.

Attack

This indicates how quickly the range is removed, or in other words, how quickly the gate opens to allow sound to come in.

Hold

This is the amount of time (in milliseconds) that the gate will stay open after the sound drops below the threshold. Normally, the gate should close as soon as it dips beneath the threshold. But if that were the case, all captured sounds would be very choppy and would lose their sustain and decay. The hold value allows more of the wanted, natural sound to come through. Think of it as a pause before the gate closes.

Decay

Similar to the hold value, the *decay* indicates how long it will take before the door closes. But, unlike hold—where the gate stays completely open to allow all sound through—the decay door closes over the entire length of the decay value. The result is a sound that trails off for the set period of time, creating a smooth, instead of abrupt, ending to the sound.

Editing

The function of *editing* cleans up the tracks' *staccato* or intermittent sounds, like that of the kick, snare, and toms. Sometimes editing is used to omit an instrument not being played for an extended period of time, in order to make more room for one that is (i.e., the hi-hat).

The problem with editing is that it causes abrupt endings to sounds, and therefore needs to be tempered with fades or gating, and/or reverb.

Reverb

Reverb is used on accent microphones to reduce the "direct" sound and restore the balance with the room microphones. *Room reverb* is the least noticeable, while *plate* and *hall reverb* are more extravagant. Almost any reverb, that has a shortened decay time, however, will sound more "natural" and less noticeable.

Reverb can help with imaging and also fill space when the drums sound too "dead"—a typical problem with slower tempo music. Acquiring a good-quality reverb is also less expensive than booking time at a studio with a professional room sound. Also, reverb can be altered and modified easier than the natural room ambience. Reverb can also be applied in different amounts to each of the different instruments.

Okay, you should now be ready to "read" the settings for these processors that I've depicted in the illustrated figures throughout this book.

Putting It All Together to Use This Book

Since drums are some of the most complex of musical instruments, I want to start the subject of recording them simplistically. I'm going to begin by using only two basic room microphones. Once I've demonstrated how to get decent sounds with them, I'll incorporate isolation/accent microphones for the individual drums. I'm also going to get into different sound options for the kick and snare, as well as miking techniques and general tips for getting an overall drum sound for a particular groove.

Chapter 8 provides examples of three different stylistic grooves, the settings for which I will go through step-by-step in order to demonstrate how you can get a finished drum sound for a particular style.

I encourage you to use the original sounds provided on the accompanying CD as guides for your dry sounds, as well as the processing settings as catalysts for your own ideas. I've included illustrated plug-ins for all of the discussed signal processing, so that you can try the same settings and adjust from there. I know how improbable it is that everyone owns vintage outboard gear and microphones, so I deliberately chose good, widely available, affordable gear; I hope that doing so will prove that you too can record drums with great results. Knowledge, an experimental spirit, and your own creativity are the most crucial tools for getting a quality recording.

Recording with Basic / Room Mics

Mic Placement for Maximum Effect

Even if you only have two microphones, you can still capture the overall drum sound as heard in the drum room. In the engineering world, these mics, set up as in Figure 40, are usually referred to as basic room mics.

Fig. 40 – Room mic setup

The quality of the sound captured with room mics is heavily dependent on the room acoustics and the sound of the drum kit in general. For the examples heard on the accompanying CD, I recorded in a large, professional tracking room. The dimensions were roughly rectangular (about 40′ wide by 70′ long by 20′ high). The room is fairly "dead," meaning that the walls and ceiling are treated with soundproofing to absorb most sound reflections. The floor is wooden, which adds some nice overtones to the drum sounds before they get absorbed into the walls and ceilings.

Some of the rooms that I have tracked in were, due to their marble floors, glass walls, and tile ceilings, very *reflective*—the material composition of such rooms cause sound waves to bounce or reflect rather than be absorbed. If done professionally, reflections will enhance the acoustic quality of the room. The sounds created by reflections are unique and specific, however; so if you are considering including them in your recording, make sure they are of a desirable color, as they will be almost impossible to remove once captured.

If you are not, however, recording your drum sounds in a professionally built room, I recommend that you pad or otherwise deaden the walls and/or ceilings in order to remove any unwanted reflections. You can do this by hanging carpeting, blankets, foam padding, etc. wherever you can. In this book, we will focus on capturing only the overall drum sound, versus any enhanced "ambience", like reflections.

Your room microphones should be *condensers*. Condenser mics are ideal for room microphones because they are sensitive to nuances and react more quickly to percussive sounds than dynamic microphones. And because the mics will be placed away from the drum kit, there is no need to worry about overloading or distorting the microphone. I used a matched pair of Audix SCX 25 microphones. Figure 41 illustrates the mic placement I used—each about 15' away from the drum kit and about 30' apart from each other (with the drums in the middle).

NOTE: Later, when listening back to the recording of the drums, you will pan the sounds from left to right in order to ensure your recording's degree of balance. It should be obvious that the hi-hat is on one side, the ride on the other, and the toms arranged from smallest to largest (with the smallest being on the hi-hat side, the largest on the ride side). Panning can be "observed" from two "perspectives." Some engineers prefer to pan the drums as if he or she were the drummer, and others pan as if they were in the audience. The first method is known as the drummer's perspective, the latter, the audience's perspective. Listen to your reference CDs for examples of, and in order to match, the panning. We will talk about panning and perspective later in the book; for now, the most important thing to be aware of is that the drums are a stereo instrument and sound best when panned in a stereo image.

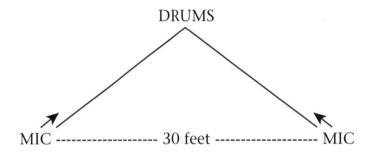

Fig. 41 – Mic placement for matched pair of condenser mics

Notice that the drum kit and mics in Figure 41 form a triangle. Because we want to make sure to capture a balanced, stereo image of the drums, we place the mics to the left and right of the kit, and the same distance from the center of the kit if possible. For my recording, I placed each mic on a stand about 6' in height.

NOTE: In a "dead" room, placing the mics a little higher (another 2–4') will likely bring out the cymbals a bit more, which could be detrimental to your overall sound. I really try to avoid accenting the cymbals; they're always loud enough anyway when picked up in the room mics, with maybe the exception of the ride cymbal. This point may also help to illustrate why multiple mics are usually used when recording drums—the more mics you have, the more control you have in accenting each or any particular drum within the overall sound.

When listening to the drum sounds picked up by the two mics, they should sound "natural." Listen to TRACK 03 for an example of the sound you want to capture with the room mics facing the kit. If you are trying out different mics to act as your room mics, I recommend choosing the pair that most closely captures what you hear naturally from the drums when standing in the drum room.

NOTE: If you'll also be using overhead microphones, don't go with the "brightest" sounding room microphones. Choosing "darker" sounding mics will provide more space in which to combine the room and overheads, without getting too much cymbal—which could drown out the rest of the drum sounds (that's why I chose the Audix mics).

Since the room mics, placed as described here, will create a stereo rendering of the drum sounds, I prefer to use a pair of identical mics, as opposed to mixing and matching different mics. Using non-identical room mics on either side of the kit may result in the capturing of lop-sided sounds—definitely not something I prefer. Any medium- to large-diaphragm microphones, which feature cardioid or omni-polar pickup patterns, will do.

NOTE: Because we are trying to get more overall drum sound without surface reflections, a cardioid-pattern mic will work best. Omnis are great when the room itself has a great acoustic quality, but because I'm going to assume that you are recording drums in a project studio environment, I suggest using a cardioid pattern to be safe. Your ultimate choice will obviously be dependant on your budget and the equipment that you currently own. Every popular manufacturer—AKG, Neumann, Rode, Shure etc.—offer mics that will work for this purpose.

Once you're satisfied with your room mic placement, turn your attention to your recording equipment.

Basic Recording Fundamentals

So, did you record good levels to your multitrack? Are you sure that your mics are facing the proper direction? These are critical questions that, if not addressed, could result in mistakes common to new recordists. Let's address these and other issues here.

Setting the Proper Levels for Recording

Every recorder has an optimum level for recording. On digital media this would be zero; on analog gear this would be between 0 and +3. By maintaining the optimal level, you'll be able to capture as much sound as possible without distorting or *clipping*. Although clipping is undesirable, you also want to avoid recording too low, which will reduce your *signal-to-noise* (signal strength relative to background noise) quality and resolution. Check your levels as you listen to the playback. The levels should be as close as possible to peaking without ever actually going over. A few decibels can make a big difference. If you're adept at using compression, you can use it to help you get more of the sound on tape without distorting or compromising the sound of the drums. When recording to digital media, I always use compression (or a limiter), but just enough to prevent clipping.

Checking the "Front" of the Microphone

Every microphone will have a "front" side, even if it's round in shape. Since it's very important to have the mics facing as intended, make sure you can find the front side of your mics. You can tell the front side of a microphone a few different ways:

1. If you have a *flat* mic (it seems to have both a front and back), look for the logo, or other imprinted symbols (like the polar pattern) on one side. This will be the front side. However, if the mic features writing/graphics on both sides:

2. Look at the pin connectors (where you actually plug the cable into the microphone). They are arranged in a triangle. The triangle's peak (the single pin), will point to the backside of the microphone, and the base (the double pins) will point to the front.

3. Do a vocal check by talking into each side, and listen to which side gets louder when you rotate the mic. If you keep your volume consistent while maintaining the same distance between yourself and the grill as you turn the mic, you should hear a difference in volume between the different sides.

Headroom / Normalization

If you are recording to a digital multitrack, then now is the time to determine and take advantage of any unused *headroom* (the "space" above the normal operating level where peaks are permitted to pass undistorted), which is analyzed through the computer function called *normalizing* (literally, adjusting the peak volume of a selection to a known value). When you set levels in the digital realm, you usually play it safe and avoid recording so hot as to peak. Ideally, you would set your levels so that the loudest incidence of the drum performance peaked at an even "0." But in reality, because you've set your levels to safely include the highest peaks, it's likely that the loudest incident will actually fall just below your 0 setting. This difference, between the loudest peak and the 0 setting, is the unused headroom. To illustrate, let's say that the loudest peak came in at 3 dB. That peak then becomes the set point to which the normalizing function raises the whole track. In this case, the whole track is raised up 3 dB, but the dynamic differences between the louder and softer sounds remain unchanged. Normalization should not be confused with compression, however. None of the sounds are getting compressed; they are simply being brought up to their optimum recorded level.

If you have a computer software multitrack or hard disc recorder, you should have access to the normalization function (consult your user's manual). Take a look at the waveform of a stereo drum recording featured in Figure 42:

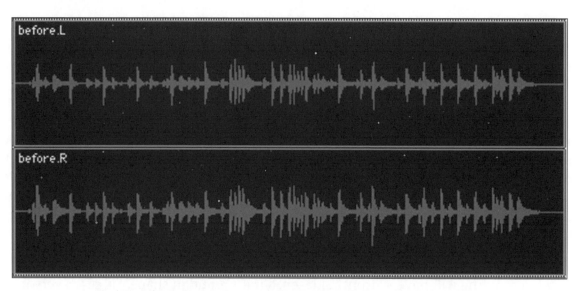

Fig. 42 – Waveform before normalizing (indicating unused headroom)

Notice how much unused headroom there is. The highest peak should be touching the edge of a region.

Figure 43 illustrates the waveform after normalizing:

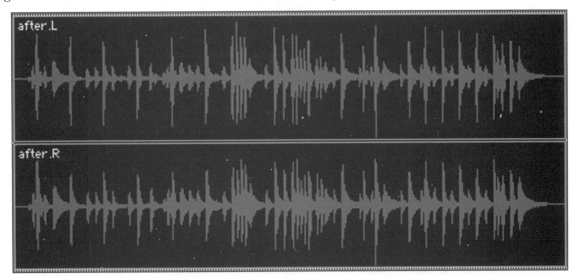

Fig. 43 – Waveform after normalizing

The relation between each of the peaks is still the same, but the overall level has been increased to take advantage of the unused headroom.

What you really gain from normalization is more audio to work with. Take a listen to the first half of TRACK 04. The first segment is the drum track before normalization. If your CD player has a level meter, watch it while playing this track. Notice how low the meters are. Also, listen to the amount of volume coming out of your speakers. Now compare this with the second segment on TRACK 04. Notice the peaking point on your CD meter. Notice also the how much fuller—and louder—the drums sound.

NOTE: Levels are crucial to the quality and resolution of your recorded sound—especially if you are recording to a digital medium. Therefore, if you want to increase volume, doing so may not be as simple as bringing up the faders. There are many ways to increase volume—fader gain, normalizing, EQ, compression, limiting, etc—and for each there is an appropriate time and place. So for the time being, just follow my lead until you find your own way of dealing with proper volume settings.

Changing Microphone Angles

Okay, if you've done everything thus far correctly, it is now time to judge the basic sound quality before we alter it. Some of you will be happy with the sounds achieved with two mics (or if you only have two mics to work with, you may have no choice but to be happy!); others will be ready to incorporate their additional microphones. However, the remainder of this chapter will be dedicated to the recording of a finished drum sound using two mics. But for those of you anxious to move on, I suggest that you still read the following sections, as their coverage on improving/altering the quality of room sounds are useful with any number of mics.

Since your particular drum kit and drum room feature variables too numerous to presuppose and address in this book, I am going to discuss some specifics for changing an overall drum balance/sound.

To illustrate ways in which you can change your mic angles, I'll talk about how to assess your cymbal sounds as an example. Are they too bright for you? If so, try turning the mics around, so they're facing away from the drum kit (see Figure 44). This should lessen the brightness. However, this mic placement may also make the other sounds a bit duller, too, so listen carefully before you decide. Also realize that, because the direct reflections from the drum kit will no longer be hitting the microphones, you will need to increase your recording levels accordingly.

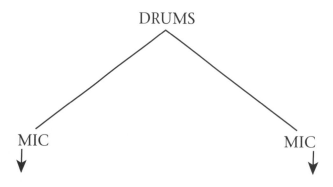

DRUMS

MIC   MIC

Fig. 44 – Mic placement: facing away

Maybe this new mic placement was a bit too drastic for your drum sound goal. Try facing the mics straight up at the ceiling; doing so will eliminate the mics' direct contact with the drum waves, but bring back a bit more brightness. Notice how this mic configuration does not make the cymbals brighter than our original mic placement (TRACK 03). That's because, even though the microphones are pointed up, they won't pick up any additional high frequencies. What they will pick up is more resonance than if the mics were facing away, but fewer direct waves than if facing toward the drums. Listen to TRACK 05, which has examples of both mic options (facing away and facing the ceiling).

If your drum room is just not sufficient for miking at a distance, try placing the drums behind the drummer, as shown in Figures 45 and 46. Doing so will create a tighter sound, which will also remove some of the unwanted "roomy" sounds produced by the kit.

Fig. 45 – Mic placement: behind the kit

Fig. 46 – Mic placement: behind the kit

Continue assessing each of your kit's drum and accessory sounds by trying various mic placement angles until you get the recorded sound you desire.

Using Your Sound Processors

Using Compression

Okay, let's address the impact of your drum sound. Listen to the last segment of TRACK 05. Does the drum sound seem somewhat small and thin? This is a basic problem that is usually due to the room itself: it may either be too small in size for good resonance, or it has been dampened, which causes a tight, but small, drum sound. The first thing to try is the addition of compression, which will sustain the drums' sounds, help bring out their resonance, and make them seem larger and more ambient. Listen to TRACK 06, on which, in addition to placing the mics facing up, I've added compression. Notice how the drums now sound bigger?

Figure 47 shows the compression settings that I used to create that sound:

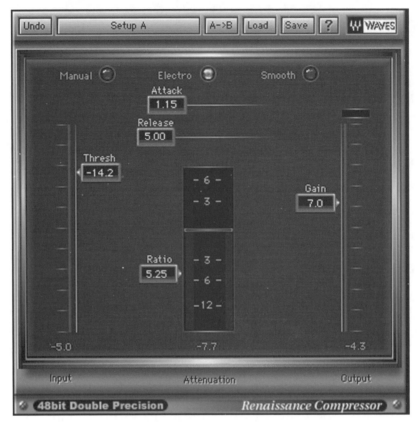

Fig. 47 – Settings for Track 06: compression

Every compressor will sound different, but start by trying the settings shown in Figure 47. The ratio, attack, and release parameters shown are settings you can try as well; but in order to duplicate the same amount of compression reduction, you will need to adjust your threshold setting until the readout of reduction shows 7 dB at the most. My threshold ended up at –14 dB, but yours will be different. All you need to do is adjust the threshold (starting from a higher setting and gradually lowering it to negative numbers) until your gain reduction meter show a 7dB reduction at the highest point. This 7 dB peak amount of compression allows you to increase the output gain by 7dB without fear of raising the level too high, and thus clipping.

If you really listen carefully to TRACK 06, you'll notice that the compressor is softening the attacks of the kick, snare, and all the other drum hits. This is because I have a "fast attack" setting on my compressor. If you feel that the drums on this track are lacking in "punch," try the settings shown in Figure 48 instead:

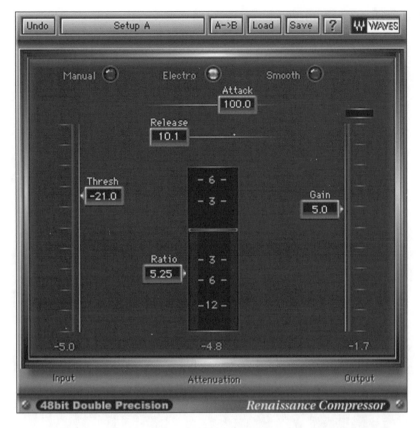

Fig. 48 – Settings for Track 07: compression with attack

Now listen to TRACK 07, then compare it to TRACK 06—can you hear more "attack" from the drum hits on TRACK 07? You should. This is a result of my having slowed down the attack setting on my compressor, so that there is a 100 ms delay before the compression will "react" to the sound. This means that the peak or punch of the sound initially gets by the compressor, which, at the time set, turns on to "tighten" whatever sound is still above the threshold, and then brings it back down under control.

Too Much Compression

Notice, especially, that I kept the release short. When the release is long, the compressor removes much of the sustain, because it does not shut off when the sound becomes quiet and falls below the threshold. This would also smooth out and tighten the drum sounds if they were ringing too much, which they aren't. Whenever I have a room that has been dampened, the issue is always a lack of sustain, not an excess.

Listen to TRACK 08 for an example of a long release, the settings for which are shown in Figure 49.

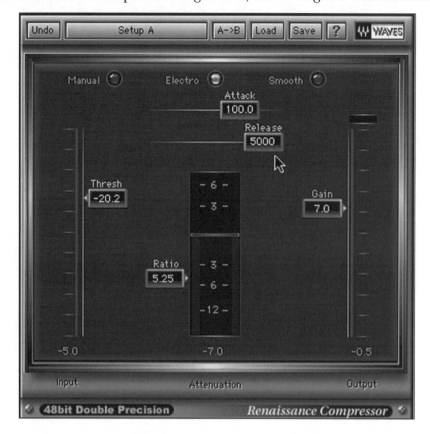

Fig. 49 – Settings for Track 08: long release

This should actually sound very close to the original drum sounds—or like the last segment of TRACK 05—but also "tightened" or "squeezed" at points. A "tight" sound is okay, but a "squeezed" sound is not so desirable. You will actually hear the sounds dip, or reduce, very quickly for an instant or longer. This happens because, when the release is too long, the compressor does not let go of the sound soon enough, so it continues to reduce the peak (even after it was a peak), and the resultant drop in volume is heard as a quick, noticeable dip. You may have heard this phenomenon on the radio or TV during a live broadcast, for which there is often so much compression and long release settings that, when the compressors do kick in, you hear them. But, as recordists, our objective is to "hide" the compression from the average listener—to add such processing "behind the scenes," so our sound modifications are undetectable. Your "concealing the evidence" here is much like what the moviemakers do when they use computerized effects that appear real, or what stuntmen do when they indiscernibly stand-in for actors.

Using EQ

Let's move on to equalization. When I want to get a stereo image of the drums, and I use an EQ, I have to remember that any changes made will affect the entire drum set's sound—not just a single drum. I can, however, maximize the effect on a single instrument while minimizing it on others, if I know how to target the right frequencies.

Let's start by making the whole room sound a little less "woofy" (sorry about the crazy adjectives, but that's how to best describe sounds). Room sounds, even when fairly tight or dead, will still have a "muddy" or "woofy" sound quality, which may mask the kick, toms, and snare attacks. One way to remove this type of overtone is to set your EQ as shown in Figure 50:

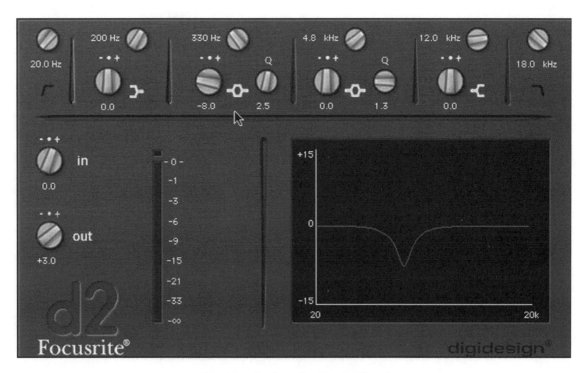

Fig. 50 – Settings for Track 09: EQ

Listen to TRACK 09. Compare it to your original, pre-EQ track. Notice how the snare pops out every time it hits, and how the kick has more emphasis? Listen to the toms. Notice how they are more pronounced? The downside, however, is that they are less "round" sounding. The decision here is yours; if you want that round, kind of muddy tone, then leave the 330 Hz settings as is. But if you're trying to get more clarity or punch, remove some of this and check out your result.

Usually, everyone's first thought is, "What should I boost?"; but the important thing here is that I did not add any frequencies. I believe in separating and removing unwanted frequencies before I begin to add or augment—like cleaning up your mess before bringing in more stuff.

Putting EQ and Compression Together

Let's listen to both processors being used simultaneously. I am going to place the compressor before the EQ so that the order is:

$$\textbf{Compressor} \longrightarrow \textbf{EQ}$$

I'm going to use the EQ setting from Figure 50, (that was used to get rid of the "woofy" sound); but, in order to remove a bit of the harshness of the cymbals, I'm going to remove 4 dB, between 4 KHz and 5 KHz, with a Q of 2, as in Figure 51:

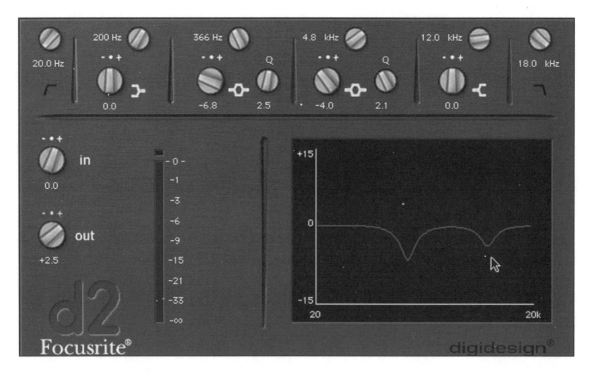

Fig. 51 – Settings for Track 10: EQ to remove harshness

The compression setting is that from TRACK 07 (the one that allowed a bit of the attack to punch through). Listen to TRACK 10, which features "bigger," or more resonant, drum sounds without the muddy mid tones. Did you notice, however, that the cymbals became louder (because of the compression) and sharper (because the EQ took out the muddy drum frequencies)? This seemed a bit too much. Notice how the cymbals are overshadowing even the snare drum in level. Listen to TRACK 11. To correct, I chose to remove some of the harsh frequencies around 5 KHz (there are several ways to solve this problem, but I'm sticking to the simplest solutions for the moment).

Using Reverb

When we compressed the drums (TRACK 10) in order to make them sound "bigger," they also became less "tight." That's because, when we used the compression to bring out more of the sustain, or natural ring of the instruments, we also lost control of the clarity.

To remedy this, we can add reverb, instead of compression, in order to create the impression of a "bigger space." Because we've chosen to deaden our room, increasing resonance naturally is a somewhat impossible option. But reverb is a separate feature that I have control over. With it I can create the kind of room that I would have liked to recorded the drums in, but didn't have the time or resources. Even if the room itself in which you record is "dead," reverb allows you to overcome that limitation, and even virtually change its settings from song to song. And with the amazing plug-ins available now for the computer, digital reverb does not sound so artificial. (My favorite plug in is Altiverb. It is the closest thing I've heard to natural reverb, as far as plug-ins go.)

Listen to TRACK 09, which features a dry, tight, room sound. Now I'm going to add a room reverb. Listen to TRACK 12, which sounds neither like a huge hall nor a plate. Nor is it also artificial sounding. But it does sound like I recorded the drums in a different room. This is the real beauty of multitrack recording: the ability to change things after they've been recorded.

Okay so what kind of reverb did I use?

Fig. 52 – Settings for Track 12: room reverb

Figure 52 shows the settings I used for TRACK 12, which is a simulation of a stereo room reverb with the dimensions as shown. But that wasn't all that I did. Because reverb is naturally a bit dull (except for plate reverb), I added the EQ shown in Figure 53 to the reverb to take out some of the low-end, and added a touch of brilliance as well.

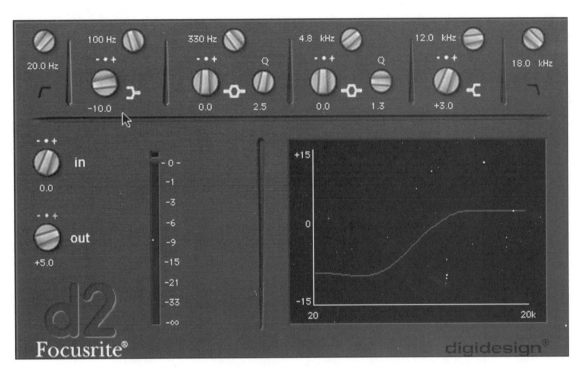

Fig. 53 – Settings for Track 15: EQ on reverb

The first segment of TRACK 13 is what the reverb sounded like before I added the EQ, which is just the reverb without the "dry" sound. By itself, the low-end sounds nice and full, but it doesn't help the original track sound more natural. Also, low-end gets muddy real quickly, so I need to be careful that I leave space in the low-frequency spectrum to share with some of the other instruments.

Now listen to the last half of TRACK 13. This again is just the reverb, but thinned out a little using the EQ setting (See Figure 53). Notice how the instruments remain tight.

So what if you want it to sound a bit bigger still? This would move us into using *hall* reverb instead of room reverb. Again, the objective is to get the drums to sound as though they were recorded in a bigger space. We're not going for an "effect"—just the impression of a "roomier" recording space.

Listen to TRACK 14 to hear the effect of hall reverb. Figure 54 shows the hall simulation settings.

Fig. 54 – Settings for Track 14: hall reverb

If the sound gets any bigger, it will begin to lose its clarity. So, for now, I'm going to hold these reverb settings.

We're now to a point where, if we want to modify the drum mix, we'll need to start adding additional microphones.

Drum Components

The following sections discuss each drum's sound characteristics, best mic choices and placements for accentuating these characteristics, and other considerations that you should be familiar with before you begin recording with individual accent microphones.

Kick Drum

Basic Sound Properties

Panning: When recording or mixing the kick, it is usually panned center (to complement the bass guitar that normally accompanies it) in the mix.

Volume: To start, the volume should be about the same as the snare (but can be louder or softer if the type of groove and style of music call for it).

Frequency Ranges: The kick has body and fatness between 80–120 Hz. The lower the frequency, the farther away from the speaker it develops. This means that if you sit very close to the speakers, you'll notice much less of the 80 Hz frequency than if you back away ten feet.

Take care when adding low-end to the kick; make sure your speakers can reproduce those frequencies, or you won't accurately hear what you are adding. Also, adjust the volume from moderate to loud, in order to hear what the low-end will end up sounding like. I normally mix consistently at a soft/moderate volume and then crank it up to get a reality check on the bass and treble. Don't worry about listening for bass at soft levels; there isn't much occurring at low volumes anyway.

A double kick gets muddy if you add too much low-end; so again, decide on a sound appropriate to the groove and style instead of attempting to boost everything in each sound.

The kick has resonance, or "live" sound between 700 Hz and 1 KHz. To tighten up the kick, reduce this range. Do the opposite to add more "live" sound.

The kick has attack—the sharp sound produced by the beater on the head—between 4–7 KHz.

The kick has clarity and definition without harshness between 10–12 KHz. When the kick starts sounding dull, and you want to bring it back to life, boost this range.

Padding

Let's talk about a crucial accessory that impacts the recorded sound of your kick drums: padding. I'm going to add a Velcro pillow padding that can be positioned inside the kick and will stay in place while played (for the longest time, I used bricks, mic bases, even a fire extinguisher a few times to keep pillows or padding inside the kit). It is crucial that the padding stay in place because it must remain in alignment with the drumheads in order to be effective. When the padding touches the beater head, it drastically deadens the attack of the sound; when the padding touches the front head, it helps reduce the hollowness of the drum. The majority of the padding should sit inside the drum to reduce the ringing of the shell, which results in a "deader" or "tighter" sound. A tight sound will have more punch and retain its clarity in an overall mix. It will also have more "impact" or quick low-end (what I refer to as "oomph").

Listen to the first segment of Track 15 for an example of a kick drum with padding, verses the second segment, which features one without. The mic (a dynamic Sennheiser 421) and mic placement are exactly the same in both cases.

Notice how hollow the kick sounds without the padding; the extra ringing sound actually takes away from the overall impact of the kick. To me, it sounds a bit loose and sloppy—like a big basketball being bounced in an arena. Experience has taught me that, when it comes time to mix the drums, that sound is going to be difficult to work with, especially if trying to imitate the kick sound on my reference CD. Listen to your reference CD. Is the kick drum tight and punchy? If so, use padding on your kick to duplicate this sound.

NOTE: Don't get too ahead of me here—the tight kick sound you just heard is neither finished, nor was it recorded with the mic or placement of choice. I just wanted to demonstrate what a huge difference padding can make. Be patient and go through this book thoroughly. The tracks that accompany it are to be followed and compared to better understand the changes that take place and the progress made on the way to a professionally finished sound. I am going to give you examples of what to do and what not to do, so follow along and don't skip any sections the first time you read through the book (that's right; the first time!), as it should take you a few times through the book in order to really absorb everything.

Now that you're familiar with the difference between a padded and un-padded kick sound, let's see if you can hear the difference between microphones.

Mic Choice and Placement

Typically, the kick drum is miked up with a dynamic microphone placed inside the drum. If you use a condenser microphone, it would typically be placed outside the drum. The closer to the inside head the mic is placed, the more the attack will increase, and more the low-end will decrease.

Fig. 17 – Kick drum

I am going to show you how to isolate the kick drum first. We are going to use a separate microphone and place it in one of three locations, as shown in Figures 18–20, below:

1. Just inside the drum:

Fig. 18 – Mic placement: kick (inside drum)

2. Far inside the drum, close to the beater head:

Fig. 19 – Mic placement: kick (close to beater head)

3. Just outside the kick drum:

Fig. 20 – Mic placement: kick (outside drum)

Each mic location will produce a different sound quality from the kick. Make note, though, that you can only place a microphone inside the kick drum if the outer head has a hole in it. Traditional jazz drum sets typically do not have a front-head hole, in which case, you can only place the microphone outside the drum. But since most kick drums do have openings in the front head, I am going to proceed on the assumption that yours does, too, so I will discuss miking-up the kick as such.

So, you've already heard the Sennheiser 421, placed just inside the front head. TRACK 16 features an AKG D12 placed just inside as well.

Did you notice how the 421 captures a very mid-range-punchy, clear, and bright sound? There is still low-end, but a tight, sharp low-end. The D12, on the other hand, records a softer, duller, and deeper kick sound. The attack is more "rounded" and smooth, with a beefy bottom end. Because you may not be using the same microphones as I am here, it is important that you be able describe your own kick drum sound appropriately—even though it may sound similar to that captured by the 421 or D12, you will need to know your own sound well enough to determine the changes necessary to get from your original sound to the finished product you desire.

When the mic is moved closer to the beater head (about 2" away), you'll get a tighter, punchier response. The D112 responds with a bit more edge and brightness than the D12 without being closer to the beater head. When the D112 is placed this close, however, it emphasizes the attack of the kick even more, and keeps it nice and tight. TRACK 17 features the D112, the D12, and the 421, respectively, placed 2" from the beater head.

Again, notice the additional attack and reduced low-end that results when each of these mics are placed closer to the beater head. But the nice "roundness" of the kick is lost in this placement. More mid-range is also added, but the trade-off is the "fat" we'd get if the mic were farther away. The 421, which is inherently bright and sharp, is even crisper when close to the beater head.

You should be able to move any mic around to alter the dry, direct (that which is not picked up in other drums' accent mics) recorded sound of the kick. Don't be afraid to have a tight kick sound from your mic; you can always blend in other mics to enhance the kick's tone.

Listen to Track 18 to hear the results of one popular method for adding tone: placing a condenser microphone 1–3' from the outside of the front of the kick drum. Due to this placement, the resulting sound will lack attack and definition, but when blended with that of the kick's direct accent mic, you'll get a best-of-both worlds result. Let's listen to a mic placed 1 foot outside the kick.

The sound on TRACK 18 has plenty of tone and sustain, but may end up getting buried later on. (Again, as we move through the book you'll see how each sound affects the other sounds in a mix.)

If you have them, place both your dynamic and condenser mics on the kick drum. You can then blend the close mic (dynamic, 421) with the outer mic (the condenser, D12). You can hear an example of this on TRACK 19. The kick is played four times; the first is the 421 mic alone, the second is the NTK alone, and the final two are blends of both. Therefore, this mic configuration gives you both the attack of the 421, and the sustain and tone of the D12.

Phase Cancellation

If you have two mics and feel that your single mic is compromising your kick sound, by all means, try blending. But beware: whenever you use two or more mics picking up the same sound, you run the risk of *phase cancellation*—the loss of a signal's frequency due to the close proximity of a like frequency. This is one of the biggest obstacles when recording drums. When there are several microphones placed around a kit, even though the direct, or accent, mics are placed correctly, they are all nonetheless capturing some sound from the other drums. (This is not to be confused with the sound captured by overheads or room mics, which pick up these ambient sounds on purpose.) Please be careful to check for phase cancellation when using multiple microphones on a single drum. TRACK 20 features tracks on which I combined the D12 and the 421. On the first two segments, you will hear the kick sound out of phase; on last two segments, the mics are in phase.

The kick is thin and short when out of phase; when in-phase, all the body and fullness returned. I have always relied on my ability to detect phase cancellation by ear. You can also make use of a *phase reversal switch* (denoted with a theta, or "?" symbol), which can ensure you're in phase. You may also have heard of the *3:1 Rule*, which states that phase cancellation can be avoided by making sure that one microphone is placed three times the distance from the source as the other mic(s). However, since moving mics can induce tonal changes (not to mention gating problems), I tend to place the mics where they will sound best, and use a phase reversal switch whenever necessary. Therefore, as long as the phase remains clean, I can put all three microphones together.

Let's see if you can detect whether a sound is in or out of phase. TRACK 21 features eight kick drum hits recorded by all three—the D12, 421, and NTK—mics blended together. After the first four hits, I flipped, or reversed, the phase for the remaining four hits (phase reversal allows both the going into and out of phase). Is it the first four hits that are out of phase, or is it just the opposite?

Even if you're not sure which four are out of phase and which four are in, you should be able to hear a difference between the two groups of hits. It turns out that the last four hits were out of phase, which is why they were lacking lower midrange frequencies and some bottom end. Since this is not really a bad sound, it's hard to tell right off the bat that this is out of phase, at least without having a phase reversal switch to refer to. Therefore, always try to check the phase whenever you use more than one mic on a sound to avoid the thinner sound that will result from phase cancellation.

Some Final Considerations

Okay, I've given you some reference sounds against which to judge your dry, unprocessed kick. Now, try to determine the sound characteristics captured by your choice of microphone. The basic characteristics to be picked up are:

1. The amount of attack
2. The amount of low-end
3. The amount of resonance and sustain

Three factors determine the degree of these characteristics:

1. The type and brand/make/model of the mic
2. The placement of the microphone in relation to the kick drum heads
3. The use of multiple microphones

The following are some tips for getting some specific basic (unprocessed) sounds:

1. To get a crisper, sharper sound, move the mic closer to the beater head
2. To get a fatter sound, place a dynamic mic just inside the outer head
3. To get a more resonant tone, add a condenser mic just outside the front head

Once you feel you've gotten the best unprocessed sound possible (as in, the closest you can get to that on your reference CD), it will likely need to be tweaked with processors such as EQ, compression, and gating.

Snare

Basic Sound Properties

Panning: When the snare is panned center, it complements the kick drum in volume. Again, depending on the groove, the snare can be louder or softer than the kick, but a good place to start is at an even level with the kick.

Frequency Ranges: The top snare sounds "fat" at around 200 Hz. It has attack between 4–7 KHz, and has clarity without harshness between 10–12 KHz.

The bottom snare should be filtered between 80–300 Hz in order to remove unwanted bleed and to add clarity to the snare.

Dampening

Just like the kick drum, the snare can, and in some cases, should be dampened. The purpose of dampening the snare, however, is to get rid of the "ringing" overtones that sometimes occur. Try to detect any ringing in your snare sound. Do you notice any high-pitched ringing? If so, you can eliminate this by adhering a piece of tape, specially made plastic ring, or gel glob to the top snare. Although we have the option of removing any ringing by editing our track, I prefer to remove it from the source.

Different Snares

There are many different types of snares, which produce different sounds, colors, and tones, and require different methods of playing. Listen carefully to the natural sound of the snare before you make adjustments to the tone.

Because it would take too long to mike up all of the different types of snares, I chose three different types to demonstrate here. The first is a *Porkpie*, which has a long, looser, sustaining-type of sound. The second is a *Markley*, which has a short, tight, cracking sound. The last is a *side snare*, or as some call it, a *popcorn snare*, which is used in drum and bass music, and has a small, high-pitched tone. Listen to TRACK 22, which features one hit for each of these three snares, respectively.

Unfortunately, I've left out the *piccolo* and some other snares, but the point is that the snare is usually the drummer's choice; if you're lucky, you'll get a few snares to choose from. Some snares are loose and ringing, others are tight and short; some are thin and high-pitched, while others are deep and fat.

The Porkpie is usually the choice for ballad snare sounds, while the Markley, which has more attack, is more popular in rock, uptempo-pop, and country. The Porkpie has a very distinctive sound that is heard prominently in the mix, while the Markley is more chameleon-like. Regardless, processing permits the modification of any snare sound, with some limitations, of course. While their inherent tones cannot be changed, their color can be altered to fit different needs.

Mic Choice and Placement

The snare is usually miked up with, at minimum, a dynamic mic on top, and, if possible, a condenser mic on the bottom (to pick up the bright overtones and ghost notes).

Watch out for overloading the condenser, and make sure that you use a mic pad. Also watch out for phase cancellation (see chapter 3), which can occur whenever you use two or more mics on the same sound simultaneously.

Top Snare

The angle of the microphone effects the isolation of the sound more than anything else. I'm going to start by placing a dynamic microphone at a 45-degree angle above the top snare (see Figure 21 for an illustration of this placement), as the 45-degree angle captures fewer of the ringing overtones. Figure 22 illustrates another option, the 90-degree angle, which actually accentuates ringing overtones. But listen for the differences yourself. The first four hits of TRACK 23 were recorded with a Shure SM57 (dynamic) mic placed at a 45-degree angle. The second four hits of TRACK 23 were recorded with the same mic placed at a 90-degree angle. The same snare was used on all hits.

Fig. 21 – 45-degree angle mic placement: top snare

Fig. 22 – 90-degree angle mic placement: top snare

Can you hear the difference sounds that each angle placement captures? Regardless of the angle you choose to use, I recommend placing the mic a distance of 1–3" away (but no more than 3"). The farther away the mic, the less attack it picks up, and the more bleed from the other drums it will capture.

Because I'm using this mic as an accent mic (as opposed to a room mic), it would defeat my purposes to place it 6" or more away. If we were not using room mics at all, then this mic would no longer be an accent mic only, and increasing the distance might be necessary.

It is also important to place the mic just inside the rim of the snare—not too close to the metal rim, which will cause an unpleasant sound, nor too far toward the middle, which runs the risk of being accidentally struck by the drummer (consequently ruining the sound and possibly your microphone). Also, ensure that the mic does not actually touch the snare drum at any time. If you're using a stand, the vibrations from the kit could cause it to droop during recording; so keep an eye on the snare mic from time to time.

Using a Condenser on Top

While the above examples were recorded with a dynamic mic, you could also use a condenser microphone on the top of the snare. You will most likely need a pad in order to do this, though. A *mic pad* is a switch located on the microphone, or an insert that is screwed into the microphone diaphragm in order to reduce the input signal. Remember, condenser microphones are very sensitive and have a tendency to overload, or distort, when placed very close to a loud sound (like a snare). Pads usually come in 10, 15, or 20 dB increments. I have found that a 10 dB pad is usually necessary in order to keep the mic from distorting. Also remember that some snares are louder than others, and for the loudest—metallic snares—I've found that a 20 dB pad is needed. Figure 23 illustrates the use of a condenser mic on a top snare:

Fig. 23 – Condenser mic placement: top snare

To hear the difference between the sound of a condenser mic and a dynamic mic, listen to TRACK 24, which features an AKG 451 placed at a 45-degree angle. Notice how the condenser produces softer and smoother sounds than the dynamic. It doesn't have the "crack" that the dynamic has, but rather a "poof" kind of sound.

Having these two distinctly different mic sounds to choose from, you will be better prepared to record most styles of snare sounds. I realize, however, that you may not have both types of mics at your disposal; so, when we get to the section on blending in the snare, my examples will incorporate a dynamic mic (which I'm assuming is the mic you have).

Bottom Snare

In addition to miking-up the top snare, you can also mic up the bottom. This is done by placing the microphone (use a condenser, if possible) underneath the snare, at a 45-degree angle, and about 4–8" away (see Figure 24). Try to avoid placing the mic right under the metal snare attached to the bottom rim. (If necessary, ask the drummer to rotate the entire snare drum, or approach the snare from a different angle.) If you are using a condenser, watch the overloading that can happen from using such a sensitive microphone—I prefer to use a 10 or 20 dB pad in order to avoid this problem. If you don't have a mic pad, you'll have to back the mic even away farther, which may cause it to lose the isolation and its relative usefulness.

Fig. 24 – 45-degree mic placement: bottom snare

The purpose of miking the bottom snare is to pick up the actual "snare" sound, which is the "rattle" that you hear when the snare is hit. This rattling is picked up to some degree by the top mic, but often needs to be emphasized. Because the rattle has a bright quality, miking the bottom snare will help to add clarity to the entire snare sound, without the need to crank up the top snare mic's EQ. This is especially important if the drummer is playing *ghost notes*—light touches on the snare by the sticks—because these soft rolls are not always picked up cleanly by the top snare's dynamic microphone. To demonstrate, listen to the first four hits on TRACK 25 to hear the sound of a condenser mic placed at a 45-degree angle, about 4" from the bottom of the snare.

If this is the sound that I am going for, then I'll need to filter out the low-end first. Listen to the last four hits on TRACK 25: these have the same sound as the first four, but with a filter rolling off the frequencies of 200 Hz and below. Compare it to the first four hits, and it will almost sound identical; the difference, of course, occurs when the kick drum is playing along. Now listen to TRACK 26, which is just the bottom snare track, but with the filter engaged at the beginning. Halfway through the groove, the filter is turned off. You can now hear the bleed from the kick drum; but notice that the snare sound didn't change.

Okay, let's modify the bottom snare sound. You can hear the definitive difference between the sound of the snare hits and that of the ghost notes. If you want them closer together in volume, you can use compression. Compressing the bottom snare will also soften the attack sound.

NOTE: Since compression will bring up all of the lower-level sounds, it is important to make sure that you filter out the low-end before you compress.

I'm also going to increase the filter point to 300 Hz, because the compression will increase the low-end bleeding. The bottom snare will thin out a little, but the top snare will balance it out. Figure 25 shows the compression settings that I will then apply:

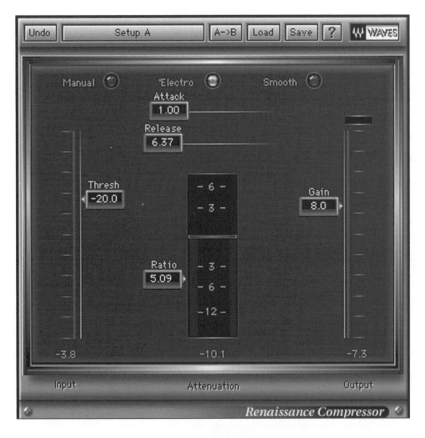

Fig. 25 – Settings for Track 27: compression

Listen to TRACK 27. Each segment features the same groove, but on the second segment, the filtering has been removed to demonstrate all of the unwanted sounds that would have bled through onto the track if left unfiltered.

If I want to soften the attacks even more, I'll use the EQ settings shown in Figure 26:

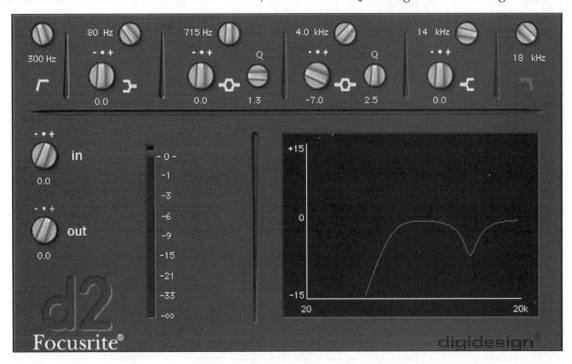

Fig. 26 – Settings for Track 27: EQ

Somewhere between 3–6 KHz is the harshness of the bottom snare. If I were to go any higher, I would just make the sound duller or less clear, but not less harsh. Some of this harshness is created when filtering the low-end. When the low-end is decreased, the mids and highs seem louder. So to compensate, we might go for more of a midrange sound by removing some of the upper mids. If you're using a dynamic microphone, then the sound might be duller to begin with, which means you may end up boosting 10–12 KHz with a shelf instead of a bell curve.

Some Final Considerations

I really recommend taking the miking-up of the snare slowly and step by step. I began with just one dynamic mic on the snare and didn't experiment with or add multiple mics until I could figure out what was missing by only using one mic. Let's recap the different functions of the three different microphones when miking a snare:

1. **Top snare/dynamic:** Adds a fat, midrange punch
2. **Top snare/condenser:** Adds a brighter, softer, puffier tone
3. **Bottom snare/condenser:** Adds a very bright tone; accents the ghost notes

The best way to approach snare miking is to first analyze what type of snare sound you're going for in order to decide which mic(s) you should use. For the examples in this book, I will be applying sound processing, so you become very familiar with how to soften up the dynamic mic or make it brighter to bring out some of the ghost notes. You don't have to use multiple mics all of the time. You may just have to spend a little more time editing and processing to get the sound the way you want it.

Hi-Hat

Basic Sound Properties

Panning: The hi-hat is normally panned to the left or the right, depending on the preference for drummer or audience perspective. It is panned anywhere from just off center to almost all the way (to either side), depending on the stereo spread desired.

Volume: The hi-hat keeps the pulse, so it should be blended just loudly enough to not lose this pulse.

Frequency Ranges: The hi-hat track picks up the bleed from the other instruments and should be rolled off between 80–300 Hz in order to minimize bleed but not adversely affect the hi-hat sound.

Mic Choice and Placement

The hi-hat should be miked with a condenser placed just above it. The mic should be angled away from the snare, to minimize bleed. Since the hat can be played closed pedal, open pedal, or open and closed with sticks, become familiar with these different sounds.

Because overheads or room mics will capture the hi-hat, but not isolate its sound, miking-up the hi-hat directly will give you control over its level in the drum mix. Nor does the hi-hat produce the loudest of sounds captured by the overheads or room mics, so relying on these ambient mics to pick up your hi-hat is not the ideal solution.

Speaking of ideal solutions, condensers are best for capturing the hi-hat, as they pick up its highs and high mids much better than dynamic mics. Figure 27 shows the ideal mic placement for the hi-hat: a 45-degree angle facing away from the snare.

Fig. 27 – 45-degree mic placement: hi-hat

The purpose of this placement is to isolate the hi-hat's sound from the snare's as much as possible, without compromising the hi-hat sound. The height of the mic is also a consideration. Remember that hi-hats open and close—they're in motion; so make sure that you place the mic at least 3" away from the hi-hats while in open position. Also remember that the hi-hats wobble when hit hard, so make sure that your mics are clear of this range of motion. And always make sure that the mic, cable, and stand are out of a playing drummer's way.

The first four hits on TRACK 28 feature closed hi-hats, and the second four feature open hi-hats.

From this, the next thing we're going to do is filter out some low-end. You can't hear it yet, but there are going to be a lot of other drum sounds bleeding into this track—which is not desirable. We'll also need to deal with something known as *proximity effect.* Any microphone placed in close proximity to a sound source will exaggerate its low-end response. The hi-hat is supposed to sound clear and not muddied up with low-end; therefore, if we filter out as much low-end as possible, we won't affect the hi-hat's overall tone. To accomplish this, I'm going to roll off everything beneath 350 Hz. Listen to the last eight hits on TRACK 28. The filter removes the proximity effect without our having to back the microphone away from the hi-hat (which would have caused more bleed). When you start to filter out frequencies higher than this, it changes the tone—which is not necessarily bad, but may not be to your taste.

I believe that, when using accent mics, it is crucial to consider how an individual drum sound will ultimately fit in the mix. To demonstrate, consider the example heard on TRACK 29. You'll hear a basic groove with hi-hats keeping time, as captured solely through the hi-hat accent mic. The first segment of TRACK 29 features this groove without filtering. The second segment features the same groove with a filter at 350 Hz, and the removal of 8 dB at 1 KHz. This filtering removes the bleed, and the 1 KHz reduction thins out the hats for clarity and takes away some of the sound's "closeness." Listen for bleed from the other sounds. Also notice that the hi-hat itself does not change that much, but is less muddy and clear—even before having added any high-end yet.

The attack of this hat sound is right around 5 KHz. If I want a softer attack, I can reduce this frequency. (Softening the hat is not absolutely necessary; but these are the tools for doing so if you so choose.) Listen to TRACK 30. The first two closed hi-hat hits have no EQ; the next two have the EQ settings shown in Figure 28. The same goes for the open sound. Can you hear the difference?

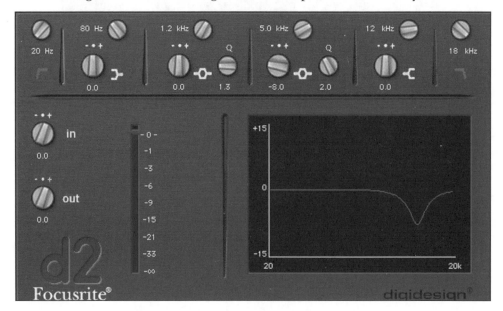

Fig. 28 – Settings for Track 30: EQ

If you need to brighten up the hi-hat, I recommend adding a frequency that is above the level of harshness associated with cymbals. Start by using a shelf at around 12 KHz, which will make the hi-hat "crisper," but not so harsh. (Just try to keep in mind that we want the hi-hat to cut through the mix, but not through your ears!) Most high-end boosting is done because the mud has not been removed. The use of a filter will help prevent the need to make the hi-hat brighter in order to get clarity. Figure 29 shows the EQ adjustments heard on TRACK 31:

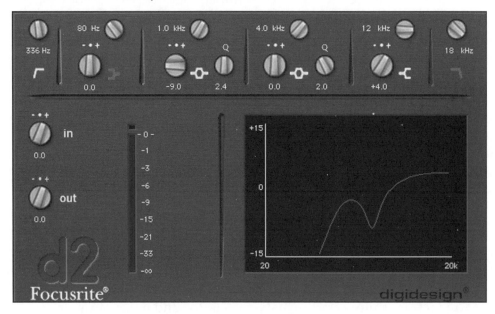

Fig. 29 – Settings for Track 31: EQ

I also have the option to put a room reverb on this in order to make the hat as captured by this accent mic sound less direct. For this groove, I would go with a small room reverb, just to add a bit of ambience or depth. TRACK 32 features our groove with some reverb added. If, however, you will be using overheads or other room mics to pick up the natural ambience of the drums, then using a reverb is unnecessary.

Toms

Basic Sound Properties

Most drum kits have between two to four toms. If there are any toms that the drummer is not using for a song, they should be removed from the kit—but make sure to keep the best-sounding ones. TOM1 is probably the most expendable, followed by the lowest floor tom.

The toms have a number of different head options. *Clear* heads (which I used for all of the examples in this book) are most common and have a snappy tone. *Batter* heads have a bit more midrange and have a generally softer sound. Batter heads are common in jazz, and clears are used for most other styles; but go with what the drummer prefers and supplies. Take care to ensure that the heads are not worn, which prevents them being tightened evenly (which may force you to resort to the messy solution of using duct tape to try to dampen any resultant ringing).

Panning: The toms are generally panned in sequence, following the hi-hat—hat, TOM1, TOM2, TOM3. If the hat is panned left, the toms should start left and go right, with the TOM3 panned almost all the way. To get the opposite effect, start right and follow to the left.

Volume: The toms fill in around the kick and snare and should be set at about the same volume as both. Depending on the number and complexity of the fills, the volume could be adjusted a bit lower to better fit the song.

Frequency Ranges: The highest tom has "fatness" between 100–150 Hz, and the other toms have "fatness" between 80–120 Hz. Long ringing can be removed between 800 Hz and 1 KHz. The attack sound can be adjusted between 3–7 KHz. Clarity sits between 10–12 KHz.

The floor tom's low-end can be boosted cleanly between 60–90 Hz. Unlike the highest tom, which is boosted between 100–150 Hz, the lowest floor tom needs to start lower. Its high-end can be boosted starting as low as 6 KHz, without adding attack, which also sits between 4–5 KHz.

Tuning

Crucial to the toms' sounds is proper tuning. Tuning will remove any wavering *overtones*—oscillations that produce an annoying "wah-wah" sound and get in the way of obtaining a nice resonance from the shell.

TRACK 33 features TOM1, tuned properly, and miked with a dynamic microphone (no processing). Notice that its sound resonates without any wavering overtones.

If you want "big" tom sounds, tune them down lower than normal—not so low and loose that they no longer resonate, but low enough to get a pitch close to the sound you want. (Sometimes I want to hear a huge *BOOM!* from the tom, but it's tuned so high that it makes a *boo* sound instead.)

Mic Choice and Placement

The toms are usually miked up with dynamic microphones, placed just above the heads. As with the snare, the 45-degree (or a little bigger) angle (see Figure 30) and the 90-degree angle (see Figure 31) are common placements for toms.

Fig. 30 – 45-degree mic placement: toms

Fig. 31 – 90-degree mic placement: toms

If you're using a dynamic mic that appears to have a front, always point the front at the toms, between a 45–90-degree angle. Try to avoid placing the mic too close to the cymbals, the snare, or the drummer's playing area. Also try not to place it too high above the tom, or you'll lose isolation and get bleed. The clip-on mics available today are great solutions to both these issues, as they are easy to place for isolation purposes and for placing out of the drummer's way.

Let's start by altering the sound of TOM1. First off, the toms will usually sound too muddy—partly due to the fact that the mics are placed fairly close to the tom heads. TOM1 starts to clear up when 300 Hz is removed (remember to be careful not to make it too thin; just clean). I could also filter out 80 Hz and below, because doing so will help clean up the track without affecting the tom tone directly.

With toms, there are three kinds of attack: 3, 5, and 7 KHz. At 3 KHz, a very "throaty" attack occurs, and you can hear the tom head better. At 5 KHz, you can hear the stick attacking the head more. At 7 KHz, you can hear a bright overtone on the attack. To add overall clarity, I'll boost frequencies 12 KHz and above; but I need to be careful, because that frequency can also boost the cymbals that are undoubtedly bleeding into these tracks.

Listen to the first segment of TRACK 34 to hear two tom hits without processing. The second segment features two hits after being processed with the EQ settings shown in Figure 32. Listen to how the EQ altered the tom sounds.

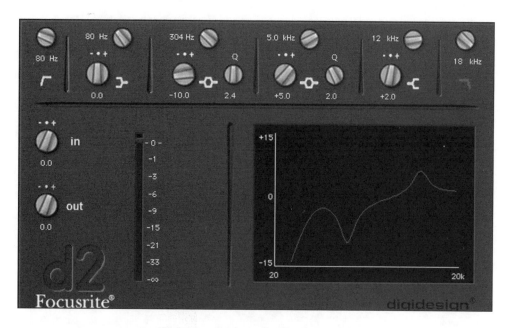

Fig. 32 – Settings for Track 34: EQ

I also want you to hear the difference between attack sounds 3, 5, and 7 KHz. The first two hits on TRACK 35 have no midrange boost; the second two are 3 KHz boosted, the third two are 5 KHz boosted, and the fourth two are 7 KHz. The different tonal qualities of each of the boosted frequencies are options to choose from, depending on how aggressive you want your toms to sound.

Another sound direction in which to take your toms is fuller and fatter, but still clean. Figure 33 shows the changes I made to the previous EQ settings:

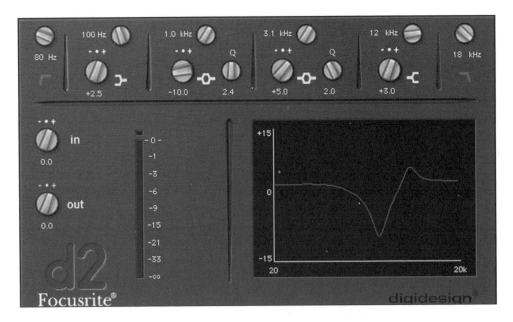

Fig. 33 – Settings for EQ: fuller and fatter toms

For this track, I also need to use a gate. Because the toms will continue to ring past their usefulness in a groove, the gate will prevent any ringing beyond a length desired. (I know that gates have sometimes gotten a bad rap when it comes to drums, but I believe that's because they are used improperly. One wrong setting can ruin the "life" of a drum sound.)

NOTE: Remember, in most grooves, there is no room for long-ringing toms, unless it's a sparse ballad played at a slow tempo.

Figure 34 shows the gate settings I used to create a short, but "natural," decay on the tom. Listen to TRACK 36, on which the first two hits were recorded without gating, and the second two with.

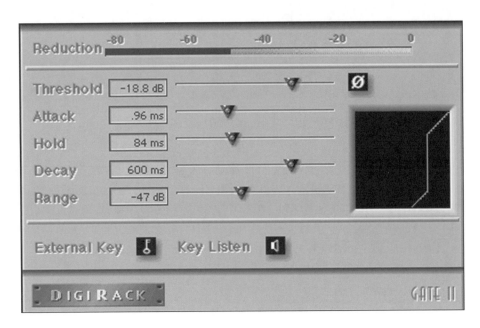

Fig. 34 – Settings for Track 36: gating

The long-ringing sound featured on this track just ends up getting lost in the groove, creating mud and bleed, and stays active in the track. Don't worry about gating out too much; we've got the room mics, overheads, and reverb to help bring back sustain if we need it.

You can apply all of the above information to any of the toms—except when it comes to EQ. That's because there is a greater frequency difference between the smallest and largest of the toms when it comes to resonance.

Let's see what can be changed on the lowest floor tom. Again, we'll get a lot of ringing that will get in the way once the drummer starts making other sounds.

NOTE: Yes, it's pretty easy to change individual sounds with processing, but it's another matter when your individual sounds include bleed from a half-dozen other sounds. But such are the instances when you'll learn the most about recording drums: once the groove starts going, you need to consider not only how an individual drum sounds, but how it sounds TOGETHER within an entire groove.

Floor Tom

Listen to TRACK 37, which features four tom hits, all captured with a dynamic mic placed 3" above the head. The first and third hits are original, dry, and unprocessed. The second and fourth hits have the EQ settings shown in Figure 35. Notice the difference in the tom sounds.

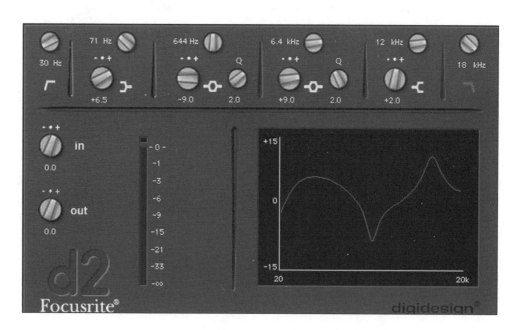

Fig. 35 – Settings for Track 37: dry and with EQ

To improve upon this sound, I'm going to add the compression shown in Figure 36 as well:

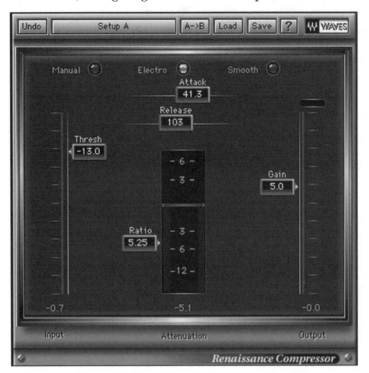

Fig. 36 – Settings for Track 38: EQ and compression

Now listen to TRACK 38, on which the hits alternate from unprocessed to processed, but this time also include the EQ and compression detailed in Figures 35 and 36. Notice how much fuller and louder the sound became with EQ and compression.

NOTE: Please remember that with the compression, the sound is actually not any "louder" in peak decibels; it just has a higher decibel average. This means that, unlike increasing volume with a fader (which could create distortion, because the peak had increased), using compression keeps the same peak, but increases the overall volume.

Overheads

Basic Sound Properties

The overhead microphones' primary function is picking up the cymbal sounds more clearly than the room mics. The ride cymbal is of special note, because it is sounds so much softer than the other cymbals, but plays a more important role. Cymbals are primarily used to accent fills and section changes. The ride cymbal is used primarily to keep time in lieu of the hi-hat. Because of this, the ride should be set at the same level as the hi-hat, or a little louder (depending on the song and musical style). The cymbal hits or crashes, however, should not overpower the individual drum sounds and should be set below the snare and kick sounds.

Since the rest of the kit bleeds into these mics, it is important to isolate the cymbals as much as possible. Gating or editing cannot be used, due to the sustaining nature of cymbals.

Panning: Overheads should be panned in relation to the preferred perspective (audience or drummer's).

Frequency Ranges: The cymbals' harshness sits between 3–7 KHz, and clarity and sparkle can be added above 12 KHz. The "live" sound of the cymbals sits at around 1 KHz.

If the overheads are not pulling double-duty as light room mics, then a roll off should be used between 80–350 Hz.

Mic Choice and Placement

Overhead configurations usually consist of two condenser microphones, in either a *spaced-pair* (see Figure 37) or *XY pattern* (see Figure 38), over the kit. They can be as close to the kit as 12", or as far as 5'.

Fig. 37 – Spaced pair mic placement

Fig. 38 – XY overhead mic placement

Both the spaced-pair and XY patterns involve crossing two microphones over the middle of the kit. The mic on the right is angled to point left, and the one on the left is angled to point right. Overhead mics are almost always condensers with cardioid polar patterns and can be placed from 1–5' feet above the kit. When using the XY pattern, an even balance is picked up, which carries a nice stereo image. The XY overheads, however, are not set as wide apart as spaced-pair, which also uses condensers with a cardioid polar patterns, and are placed at the far left and right of the kit. The spaced-pair overheads should not sit above the snare drum (to avoid more snare bleed) or the center of the kit, but rather at the ends of the kit, in relation to the cymbals. One microphone should be placed roughly in the middle of the cymbals on one side, and the other roughly in the middle of the cymbals on the other side. A wider stereo image is created with spaced-pair placement, but the balance of left to right is not as smooth as with the XY pattern.

Sometimes, overheads are used instead of room microphones. This occurs when either the room acoustics are awful, or there are an insufficient number of microphones to have both overheads and room mics. I always recommend using overhead microphones in stereo, regardless of whether they are doubling as overall drum accents, or used primarily for cymbal accents.

When used as cymbal accents, the goal with overheads is to filter out as much of the kick, snare, and toms as possible without compromising the sound of the cymbals. The first segment of TRACK 39 features a groove recorded with just the overheads miked up in a spaced-pair configuration. The first thing to do now is to filter out all the frequencies not containing the cymbals. How do you know which frequencies these are? Take a filter and sweep it from the lowest frequency on up, until you notice the cymbals becoming thinner than those on the original track. (I just listen for the ends of the drum grooves where the cymbals ring out, then quickly turn the filter on and off at gradually higher frequencies.) Now listen to the second segment of TRACK 39. This is the same track as the first segment, but with a filter rolling off 375 Hz and below, with a 24 dB per octave slope.

Notice how the kick drum has almost disappeared completely! Notice how the cymbals are "clearer" without my having added any EQ. And all we did was remove the overtones of the other drum sounds.

Now, after you have filtered out the unwanted sounds, it's time to even out the cymbals. Each cymbal has a different tone (which is desirable), but radically different volume levels (which is not desirable). I'm going to recommend using compression in order to even out the cymbals' attacks and to balance their levels with each other.

If you find that your cymbals are very harsh-sounding and take up a lot of space when too loud, compression is a must. Compression will also give the cymbals more sustain. Because cymbals, when mixed with the rest of the music, are very transient-sounding, their attack is clearly heard, but their sustain quickly falls beneath the other sounds; this makes the cymbals sound very short and harsh. The compression settings shown in Figure 39 will bring up the sustain and level out the attack, making the cymbals start out smoother and last longer. Now the overall volume of the overheads need not be excessively loud in order to be clear.

Another nice thing that compression will do, especially as demonstrated in this example, is keep the ride cymbal from getting lost in the mix. The ride has one of the softest cymbal sounds, but is a very important drum component, especially when keeping time. The accents and crashes of the other cymbals usually dwarf the level of the ride, resulting in the overheads capturing sounds too loud (crashes) or too soft (the ride). Using compression will even this all out.

When using the compressor, start out with a 5:1 ratio or so. The keys things to be mindful of here are your threshold setting and your attack and release times. The threshold should be set higher than the ride cymbal peaks. If you have a compressor with an input meter, just watch and listen for the ride cymbal in order to find the proper level.

Regarding the attack, the shorter the attack time, the smoother and less "punchy" the cymbals. For ballads and softer music, 1–20 ms creates the smoothest quality. For rock and pop, we might be nearer 50–100 ms, which will allow some of the attack to get through.

Lastly the release should be set so that it is not noticeable. When the release is set too short, you can hear the compressor turning off, as well as a steep level increase. When the release is set too long, the sustain will be removed from the cymbals. You have to really listen to set the release. Go to each end—too short and too long—so that you can hear the worst possible settings; then settle somewhere in the middle. Just try to make it release quietly, without taking away the nice decay and sustain of the cymbals.

TRACK 40 features the compression settings shown in Figure 39:

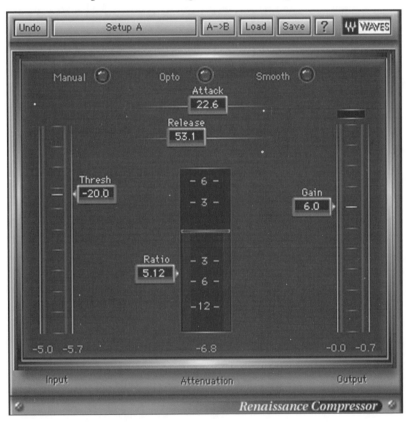

Fig. 39 – Settings for Track 40: compression

Now, before you go boosting or cutting with your EQ, I'm going to recommend that you first test how it fits in with the rest of the drums. You might need to brighten up with a shelf at 12 KHz and up. Or you might need to soften it up by removing a bit of 3 KHz. It all depends on style and the other microphone sounds.

Remember that the purpose of the overheads is too accent the cymbals, without bringing in too much bleed from the other drum sounds. Here's a good rule of thumb: to remove before you add. Even if you have to remove a bit more low-midrange in order to clean up the cymbals, that would be preferable to cranking up the high-end.

Mastering, which occurs when recording is finished, is a completely different subject; but I want to mention here that, because mastering engineers will usually add the final touches of presence to the mix, if the cymbals are too bright and loud in the mix, their hands are pretty much tied, and nothing more can be done. So take special care when recording cymbals.

This brings up another issue: how loud you make the overheads in the mix. Listen to your reference CDs to get ideas of how loud the crashes and ride should be—they are usually a lot lower than what you might expect. Really look at chapter 8, in which I show examples of how to mix three different drum grooves, and check the levels of the overheads in relation to the other sounds. Remember, keep them just loud enough to accent them.

Now listen to TRACK 41, on which I've filtered out even more (up to 900 Hz) and boosted just a little (3 dB at 12 KHz). Even though the cymbals are now thinner, they will end up sounding cleaner and clearer. Don't forget: if you are using basic room microphones, they will capture some of the tone that is missing from the overheads.

Recording with Accent Mics

As you discovered in Chapter 4, there are limitations to altering individual drum sounds with a two-microphone setup; when one aspect is altered for a desired effect, another is affected in a way not necessarily desirable. Incorporating additional, or accent, microphones, which are placed to pick up and manipulate individual drum sounds, will not only alleviate this problem, but will also allow you to further control volume, tonality (EQ), attack, panning, and isolated effects.

Adding Accent Mics to Individual Drums

Kick Drum

Let's start by adding an accent mic just for the kick. I'm going to shape this drum sound from the room sounds heard on TRACK 42's groove. Figure 55 shows the EQ parameters used on this basic sound.

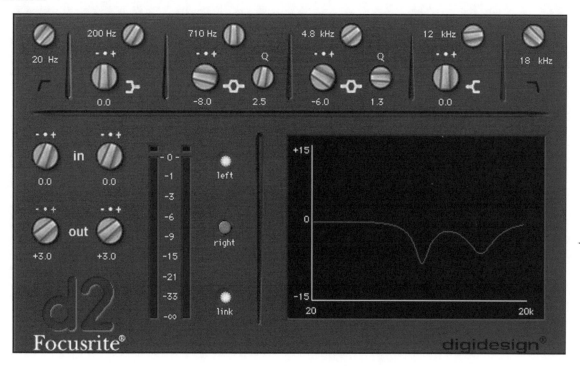

Fig. 55 – Settings for Track 42: EQ

Let's start building our drum sound.

Editing and Augmenting

One of the main objectives of using accent mics is to maximize the desired sounds and minimize the undesired, which is done with various editing and augmenting options. One particularly undesired sound is *bleed*. Bleed occurs when the accent mic picks up sounds from the kit's other drums and components (no matter how far inside the kick the accent mic is placed, it still picks up some degree of bleed). Furthermore, if we compress the signal from this accent mic, we'll bring up not only the overtones of the accented drum, but also the bleed from the other drum sounds. Since our room mics are already picking up ambient sounds, and since each accent mic is picking up its own share of bleed, unless this noise is cleaned up or eliminated, you'll end up recording it from multiple sources. The more mics used, the worse this problem becomes, unless we isolate the accent sounds.

NOTE: Another factor to consider here is phase cancellation (see chapter 3), which can occur when using multiple microphones.

Listen to TRACK 43, which is the kick with the mic placed about three inches from the inside head, and without the room sounds blended in. Figures 56 and 57 show the settings for the EQ and compression that I applied in order to keep the kick's attack clean and punchy. (And really listen for the bleed from the snare, toms, and cymbals.)

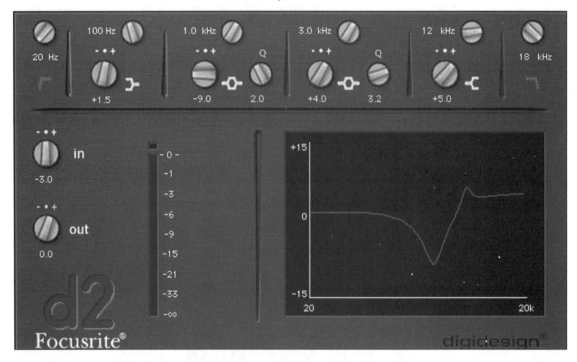

Fig. 56 – Settings for Track 43 : EQ

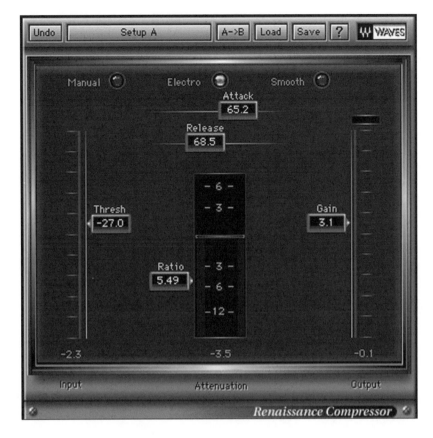

Fig. 57 – Settings for Track 43: compression

Figure 58 shows the current waveform of this kick track:

Fig. 58 – Waveform for Track 43: bleed unedited

I've labeled Figure 58's peaks with an "s" for "snare," "k" for "kick," and "t" for "toms." When I edit (cut out these unwanted parts from) this kick track, I will remove these peaks/bleed from these other instruments with my computer editing functions. The resultant waveform will look like that shown in Figure 59:

Fig. 59 – Waveform for Track 44: bleed edited

I've indicated on this graphic where the kick peaks are, but you'll notice that the snare and tom peaks are gone. Take a listen to TRACK 44 to hear what the edited track like.

If you've never heard edited drums before, TRACK 44 will sound kind of weird at first. Most of the kick's resonance is cut off, but that's okay, because I'll be bringing back some of the natural resonance through the room microphones. Notice also that I kept some of the ringing of the cymbals in a few of the kicks. If I had edited those, they would sound chopped off and very abrupt.

NOTE: This is the secret to editing. Most editing problems come from cutting off the edit too soon; and, when cutting the sounds into small chunks, you want to the edited track to be free of any pops or glitches. You want a sound that's cleaner in the end, not choppy.

TRACK 45 is TRACK 44 with the room sounds blended in. Notice how the kick sounds cleaner than it did before the tracks that were blended.

This track is now ready for the next step—the addition of reverb (the sound of reflections bouncing off of the surfaces of the room).

Snare Drum

In most cases, the snare sound picked up from the two room mics will be loud enough as is. My first goal, therefore, is to lower the volume of the overall drum sound picked as up by the room mics while maintaining the attack of the snare.

Getting a Snare Sound with Maximum Attack

In order to get the snare sound to really "crack" or "pop," I will first need to completely isolate it. I will do this with computer editing, just as I did for the kick drum. The only difference is that this time I'm going for a completely short, isolated sound—which will sound very unnatural at first.

Things to remember when editing the snare sound:

- Listen to each hit that you edit, and make sure that there are no computer noises created from your editing (i.e., pops, snaps, etc.).

- Do not allow ringing or cymbal bleed to infiltrate the snare track.

- Do not worry about the unnaturally short sound—yet.

The first segment of TRACK 46 is our raw snare track. Notice the ringing from the snare and the bleed from the other drum sounds—especially the toms and cymbals. The first thing to do is edit out these sounds. The second segment of TRACK 46 is the edited version that features the snare hit only; the ringing and bleeding are gone. And yes, the track sounds pretty weird right now, but stick with me.

Next, I will apply the EQ settings shown in Figure 60 in order to bring out the "attack" of the snare hit.

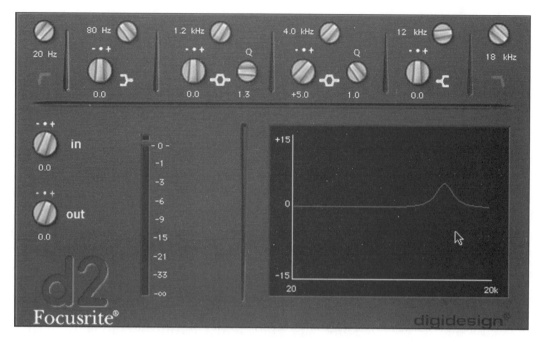

Fig. 60 – Settings for Track 47: EQ

Next, I will apply the compression settings shown in Figure 61 in order to gain focus and control over the sound. Because getting more attack is my objective here, I'll need to lessen the amount of sustain.

NOTE: The more attack, the less sustain. To augment a certain sound quality, it's obviously necessary to add the proper processing, but it's also important to remove the opposite quality in order to help maximize the result.

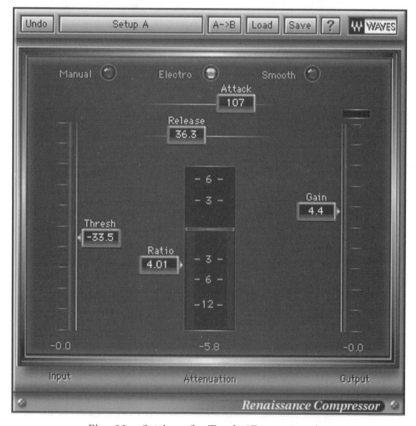

Fig. 61 – Settings for Track 47: compression

Let's hear how these two effects work to focus the snare sound and give it more "bite." Listen to the first segment of TRACK 47.

Right now, you might be freaking out because it sounds like I just ruined the snare sound, but stay with me—we're not finished yet. Now it's time to blend in the accented kick drum (TRACK 45) and the two-mic basic room sounds (TRACK 42). The result is the second segment of TRACK 47, which was obtained by a total of our four mic setup (two room, one accent on kick, one accent on snare).

The final touch is to add in a bit of reverb to mask the abrupt endings of the edited snare. The reverb setting I will use is a large room sound (to simulate a live studio space about 45' by 30'), which I will blend much lower in the mix. I'm going to try to get a good balance in the volume between kick and snare and just blend the room in enough to get the cymbals at a respectable volume. For now, the snare and kick are panned in the center, and the rooms are panned far left and right. The reverb is also panned to the far left and right, in order to add ambience and space. Since we still haven't covered hi-hats and toms, those sounds will remain unfinished here and will need to be altered later. For now, listen to attack of the finished snare sound on TRACK 48.

For learning purposes, I want to give you an example of what would have happened if your editing had been too long, since the tendency of most new recordists is to edit the snare to sound more "natural." Listen to the first segment of TRACK 49. This is TRACK 48 with both the "ring" and close bleed still present, but with the compression and EQ settings left intact.

Let's now blend the first segment of TRACK 49 with kick (TRACK 45) and basic room mics (TRACK 42). The result is the second segment of TRACK 49. Notice that the editing of the snare is obvious here. The ends sound chopped because the ringing stops too abruptly. And even if reverb were added to this mix, it would not be effective in covering up these ringing edits.

While we're at it, let's listen to the dry snare—without EQ, compression, reverb, or editing—blended in with the kick and room mic tracks. To demonstrate a greater degree of transformation, I'm even going to remove the processing that we used on the kick and room tracks. Listen to TRACK 50. You should now feel good about the progress that we are making! Compare this with TRACK 48, and notice how much we have altered the original sound.

Bottom Snare

We're not done with this snare sound yet. Because I edited the snare track to get a tight, "snappy" sound, I consequently removed the *ghost notes*—those light touches on the snare by the sticks. To regain the ghost notes, I will start by tracking the groove with a bottom snare mic. Listen to this unprocessed sound on the first segment of TRACK 51. Listen for what sounds like the light tapping of the sticks the snare; here it will sound like a little shuffle (you will need to be familiar with any drum groove you are editing to ensure that you're editing the relevant sounds).

From this, I will edit out everything but the ghost notes. This is the sound you hear on the second segment of TRACK 51. Now I'm going to add the EQ settings shown in Figure 62 in order to help it to blend in more with the top snare.

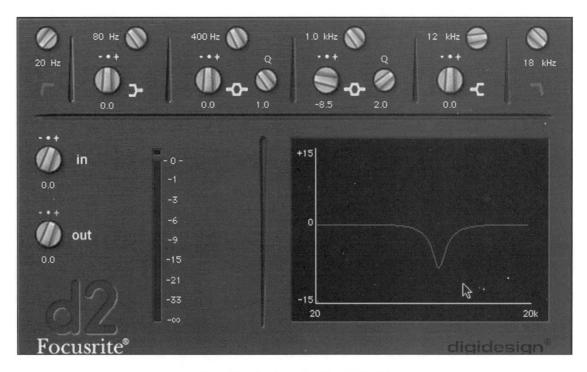

Fig. 62 – Settings for Track 52: EQ

Last but not least, I'll add reverb. I don't want the ghost notes to "stand out" as though they're separate from the drum mix; so, in order for them to fit into the overall sound, I'm going to use on this track the same panning and reverb settings that I did on the top snare (center). The finished product is heard on TRACK 52.

NOTE: Some engineers prefer the sound of bottom-snare ring, and others do not. It really depends upon drum sounds you are going for. Keep in mind that drum sounds are easily muddied when blended in with bass, guitar, vocals, etc.; hence the need for editing. In blues, classic rock, jazz, etc., the objective is not so much on tight-sounding drums as it is on those that sound natural. However, in heavy rock, pop, etc., the focus is more on fitting the drums into the whole production. The objective here, then, is to leave enough space for the other instruments to fill, separate those sounds clearly, and have the ability to change the production radically.

Getting a "Fatter" Snare Sound

Another popular snare sound is the "fat" snare. Unlike the "snappy" snare, the fat sound features rounder, fuller, and softer punches. Again, for learning purposes, let's manipulate TRACK 46 to get a fat snare sound.

The frequency at which the snare gets fuller is right around 200 Hz. I'm going to use EQ to boost this frequency according to the settings shown in Figure 63:

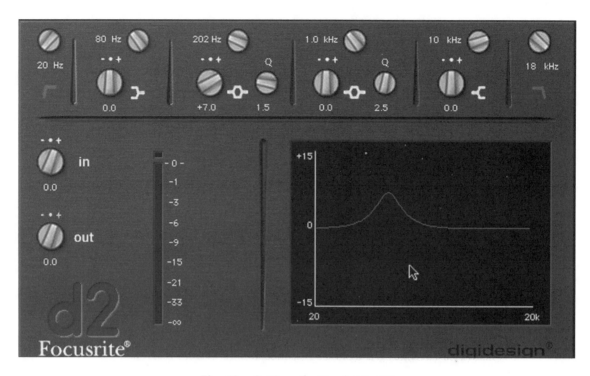

Fig. 63 – Settings for Track 53: EQ

Again, we'll need to use compression. To get the "fat" to come through, the sound needs to be focused. Figure 64 shows the compression settings I will be using:

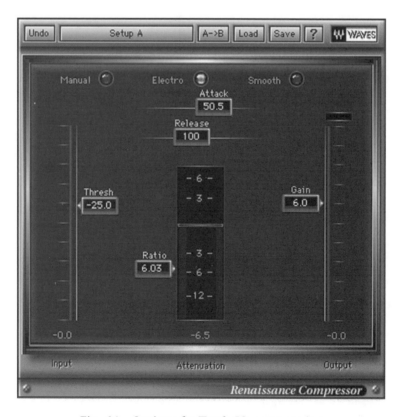

Fig. 64 – Settings for Track 53: compression

Another big factor here is the editing. If I were to edit this track as I did when going for the "tight" sound of TRACK 48, the setting will be too short to allow the low-end to resonate and become full. On the other hand, the long edit of TRACK 49, which allows the ring to come through, would be too noticeable when blended into the entire track. Because editing abruptly cuts off sound, snares with a "trail" or "fade" would sound less chopped. (For those of you familiar with crossfades, you know that I could use the computer to put them into every snare hit—but that would be a lot of work, so let's ignore that possibility for now.) Therefore, I'm going to use a gate.

I'm going to start by using the TRACK 49 version of the snare (the one with the ringing and a small amount of bleed), to which I'm going to apply a gate. I'm only going to use the gate to fade, or close, the door on the ends of the snare hits. Figure 65 shows the gate settings:

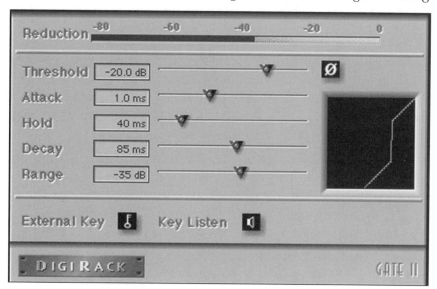

Fig. 65 – Settings for Track 53: gate

Without getting overly in-depth about gating, let me just say that it acts much like an automated cut or mute. The difference, though, is that a gated sound can be gradually cut by the set amount of *hold* (the amount of time the "door" stays completely open, allowing sound to come through) and *decay*. As the door closes, the sound diminishes—not all at once, but gradually, in even increments. We're talking about milliseconds here, but that's all it takes to subtly "fade" the ringing out of the snare, avoiding an abrupt halt. A mere 40 ms of hold and 85 ms of decay will do the job.

Listen to the first segment of TRACK 53, which features the fuller snare sound without the gate being applied. Notice the abrupt endings. Now let's apply the gating so that we can hear how it should sound. The result is heard on the second segment of TRACK 53. To hear how much thinner the unprocessed snare sounded, refer back to TRACK 50.

Extending the Snare Sound

Have you ever wondered where the engineers of '80s pop music attained those long, big, bright reverb sounds? They used an effect known as *plate reverb*, which has a bright, metallic quality. Today's processors simulate plate reverb, which is also used to stretch out the length of the snare sound without masking it. The first segment of TRACK 54 features plate reverb on the snare. Its bright characteristic makes the snare sound as though it continues to rattle past the initial hit. The key to using plate reverb here is to adjust the pre-delay to about 60 ms, meaning that the reverb will not begin until 60 ms after the snare has hit. This is a "clean" way to extend the length of the reverb without extending the length of the reverb itself. All this really does is delay the reverb by 60 ms, which is when it would have been noticed anyway. Within the first 60 ms, the listener is still focused on the attack of the snare, which would serve as a mask if I didn't create the pre-delay.

Also, when the reverb is big, like this one, I prefer to pan it in the middle—not out to the left and right. Otherwise, the reverb would not serve the purpose of spaciousness, but rather of length.

But I still use plate reverbs on a lot of snare sounds; I just adjust the decay or length in order to make it sound tighter and less dramatic. Never feel stuck with stock settings; feel free to alter them. When the accented snare track needs to blend in better with the rest of the drums, reverbs are a nice way to fool the listener into not noticing that the accent mic provided the main snare sound.

Listen to the second segment of TRACK 54. This is the same plate reverb as on the first segment, just shortened up a bit so as to blend in better. I've also reverted back to the bright, edgy snare sound, which blends better with a plate reverb. Feel free to experiment with different types of reverbs; just remember to apply the same reverb to the bottom snare as well.

Cymbals

Because the groove used on our last few tracks feature a ride cymbal instead of a hi-hat, I'm going to cover the miking-up of cymbals next. For cymbal accent mics, I am going to recommend that you use condenser microphones, and a pair of them in order to get a nice stereo image. (I often use three microphones just for the ride cymbal because it's the quietest, but most important, cymbal. But I'm going to stick to a two-microphone setup for now.)

Normally, the cymbals play the accents, but the ride cymbal is actually used to keep time. Therefore, the crash cymbals should be mixed lower in the overall drum sound, so that the ride and its rhythm are not lost. It's best to keep the ride at the same level as the hi-hat. (Most drum grooves feature hats on the verses and move to the ride for the choruses and/or bridge. Because I don't want this movement to lessen, I'll pay close attention to the ride volume.)

First, let's check out how to mike up the cymbals. One option is the XY setup of Figure 66, in which the mics are placed over the center of the drum kit, anywhere from 1–6' above the kit. The closer the microphones are to the cymbals, the clearer they'll be, and the less room sound that will bleed in. (This also ensures less of a chance of phasing problems, which was discussed in chapter 2.)

Fig. 66 – XY pattern mic placement

Basically, in an XY setup, the microphones cross each other and point to the opposite ends of the drum kit. A cardioid pickup pattern mic works best with this setup.

However, if I want a wider stereo image of the drums, I can use the spaced-pair setup, as seen in Figure 67. The height of the mics is within the same range as the *XY setup*, but the mics are placed facing the drum kit, on a slight angle, away from the toms and snare.

Fig. 67 – Spaced-pair mic placement

Let's see if you can hear the different stereo images that each setup creates. Each cymbal is hit from left to right. The first segment of TRACK 55 features the XY setup, and the second segment (after the long silence!) is of the spaced-pair. Pay close attention to the ride cymbal as well as the crash after the ride. It should be easy to hear how the XY setup sound bleeds into both speakers on every cymbal hit, resulting in a narrower image. The spaced-pair setup has a wider image, and the cymbals more obviously move across the speaker imaging. The XY setup picks up all of the cymbals better than the spaced pair, which favors the far left and right cymbals most. For drum kits with only a few cymbals, I would use the spaced-pair setup. The XY setup is best for kits with more cymbals, and for instances when each cymbal serves a specific purpose in a song, so as to pick up all of the sounds more evenly.

NOTE: Before you record, if possible, use a roll-off. A roll-off is a filter that removes low-end frequencies. Because cymbals have no audible low-end, using a roll-off will simply remove some of the bleed that comes from the other drums. Remember, regardless the setup you use, the overhead mics are still accent mics, and thus used for isolating the cymbals as much as possible. If your mic does not have a roll-off, then a filter (EQ) can be used during recording or mixdown.

Now let's hear what the spaced-pair overheads sound like without filtering out the low-end. Remember, I'm just trying to accent the cymbals; any extra drum sounds that get through are going to be unwanted. Listen to the first segment of TRACK 56. The toms and snare are coming through very loudly in these microphones. Now, if I didn't have room microphones and/or I couldn't mike up the toms with their own accent mics, then I might leave this as is. But because the overheads are dedicated to the cymbals alone, I am going to *filter* out all the low-end from 350 Hz and below. Filters sometimes have a dB/octave setting that ranges from 6–36 dB—a measurement for the slope, or how gradual the removal is. Most filters are fixed at 12 or 18 dB per octave; but I have a computer plug-in that allows me to adjust the range up to 24 dB, so I'm going to use that one. Listen to the second segment of TRACK 56, which is the same as the first segment, but filtered. Notice how the cymbals are much cleaner and clearer, and the toms and snare are now much quieter in the track.

NOTE: If you need to adjust your filters, just do this: Start by rolling off the lowest frequencies (around 60 Hz) and gradually increase the frequency point. When you reach about 200 Hz, turn the filter on/off. You will hear the other drums change in tone, but you won't hear the cymbals change at all. Keep raising the frequency until you notice the cymbals being affected—they will start to get thinner. When this happens, lower the frequency on the filter back to a setting that did not affect the cymbals. Before I recorded the second segment of TRACK 56, I kept going back and forth between the "bypass" and "on" modes in order to detect any differences in the cymbal sounds. When I was satisfied that I couldn't, I checked the frequency and noticed that it was at 350 Hz. (It's good practice to use your ears as well as your eyes!)

I'm also going to compress the cymbals, so that they are all at about the same level. Because the crashes are so much louder than the ride, I'm going to use compression to even them out a bit more, too. Figure 68 shows the compression settings:

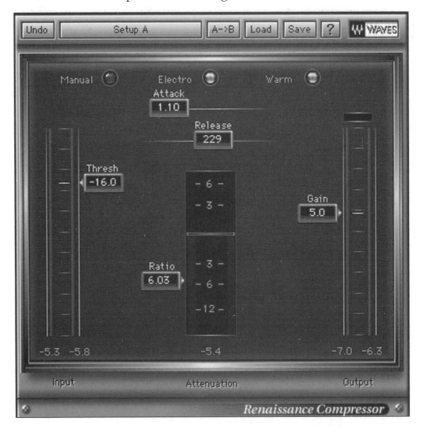

Fig. 68 – Settings for overheads: compression for cymbals

It's important here that I set the threshold higher than the ride level, as I don't want to compress the ride. I also need to watch the length of the release—if it's too short, I'll hear a "flutter" sound from the compressor; and if it's too long, I'll be squashing the sustain of the cymbals.

Figure 69 shows the filter and some additional EQ settings. I've filtered out 1 KHz to take out some of the "live" tone of the cymbals, which will help them blend better and refrain from overshadowing the other instruments.

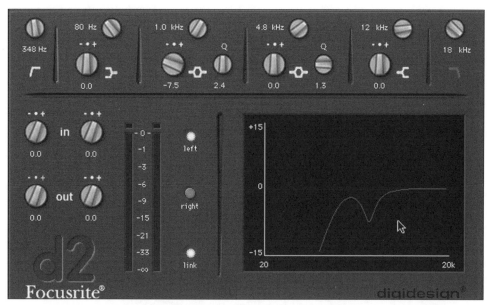

Fig. 69 – Settings for cymbal filter/EQ

Let's blend this in with the existing drum mix from our previous snare example. We'll be blending the kick, top snare, bottom snare, overheads, and room mics. I'm going to lower the room sounds, which, up until now, I've been relying on to capture the cymbals. Now they will fade into the mix and add just a bit of ambience. Figure 70 shows the fader levels for this mix.

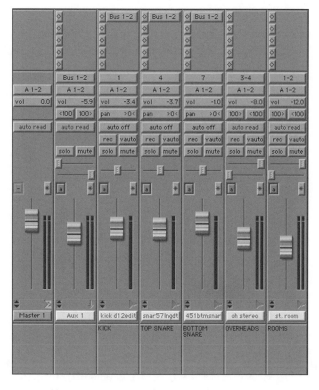

Fig. 70 – Settings for cymbal fader levels

Toms

Now that we have the kick, snare, and cymbals blended in with the basic drum sound, we need to capture the tom sounds. Because have lowered the basic drum mix (a.k.a. room sounds) as we brought up the accent mic sounds, the toms have now clearly gone way too far back in the mix. Let's discuss how we mike up and alter the toms to fit into the mix.

The toms are normally accented by placing a dynamic or condenser microphone above each drum at angles of either 90 degrees (see Figure 71) or 45 degrees (see Figure 72).

Fig. 71 – 90-degree mic placement: tom

Fig. 72 – 45-degree mic placement: tom

Dynamic mics (i.e., SM57s, Sennheiser 421s) are your best bet for miking toms, as condensers are sensitive and will pick up more high- and low-end than dynamic mics. But if you're using condensers, hopefully they're the clip-on types that attach to the rims, like SM98s or regular condensers like AKG414s.

Whichever type you use, the critical factor is mic placement. Try to place the mics so as to minimize bleed from the snare and cymbals. Also make sure that the mics do not get in the way of the drummer's sticks when the toms are hit. It's very important to ensure that the mics cannot be touched by any moving cymbals, as cymbals are usually placed directly above the toms. If you're using clip-on mics, this is not really an issue; but if you're using larger mics, like a 421, on stands, you may have to adjust the mic angle in order to clear enough room for cymbal movement.

Regarding angles—try not to point the microphone toward the snare, or especially the high tom or first tom. Because this tom accent mic usually sits directly above the snare, try to angle it toward the second tom if possible.

I'm going to use three toms for the following examples. I will call them TOM1 (a.k.a. high tom, highest pitch), TOM2 (a.k.a. rack tom, midrange pitch), and TOM3 (a.k.a. floor tom, lowest pitch).

The toms are used, in most cases, to create the fills of a groove. They can be panned in different ways, but one option is called *drummer's perspective*, which is illustrated in Figure 73:

```
L ----------------------------- C ----------------------------- R
        Tom 1              Kick    Tom 2    Tom 3
                          Snare
```

Fig. 73 – Panning pattern: drummer's perspective

The "L" is far left, the "C" is center, and the "R" is far right. On an actual kit, the first two toms sit close together, but the kick and snare are in the middle, so I don't place TOM2 there as well. I've used a clock pattern to describe the panning order below:

TOM1:	10 o'clock
Kick/Snare:	12 o'clock
TOM2:	2 o'clock
TOM3:	4 o'clock

Another panning pattern, known as the *audience's perspective*, is illustrated in Figure 74:

```
L ----------------------------- C ----------------------------- R
   Tom 2    Tom 3    Kick    Tom 1
                     Snare
```

Fig. 74 – Panning pattern: audience's perspective

The audience perspective is simply the reverse of drummer's perspective. I usually listen to my reference CD first and choose one of these perspectives based on that. I listen to where the hi-hat and ride are (usually on opposite sides of the stereo image), and then the placement of toms (either left-to-right or right-to-left). Regardless, I'm always concerned about keeping the ride and TOM3 on the same side, and the hi-hat and TOM1 on the other. Unless the drummer is using an unusual setup, this is standard panning protocol. I've worked with drummers who use multiple hi-hats and who placed their toms in bizarre sequences around their kits. I usually try to pan in their same order, either from the drummer's perspective behind the kit, or audience's in front of the kit. But I definitely avoid mixing and matching at random. Remember that the basic room mics, the overheads, and the toms all have to be panned identically, or phase and imaging problems will result.

The main purpose of using accent microphones is to get a nice, clean attack. The basic drum sounds/room mics will capture most of the decay and ambience, so I'm more concerned about getting the initial drum tone from the accents.

Tom1

TRACK 57 features TOM1 miked with a Sennheiser 421 at a 45-degree angle before any editing. In this groove, the toms are played only a few times, so I'll want to clean this track by removing the obvious bleed from the snare and the constant vibration of the shell. I will cut and edit the track so that just the five tom hits for TOM1 remain. This edit will be trickier than the snare and kick edits, because the toms will not taper off nicely at the end; plus, there is so much bleed that the cleaned-up track will probably sound edited.

Now listen to the five edited tom hits on TRACK 58, and notice that, with the last tom hit, TOM2 was allowed to bleed in. Because the drummer played the TOM2 immediately after TOM1, if I had edited out TOM2, it would have had no sustain at all. So, I in order to make the track sound less obviously edited, I left the bleed in. Did you also notice that the ends were not perfectly clean? To remedy this, I'm going to use a gate (like we did with the snare), which will remove those sounds at the end of the edits.

If I hadn't used a gate on the toms, and then tried to blend them in, the edits would have been extremely noticeable. Listen to the first segment of TRACK 59, and pay attention to these abrupt endings on the tom edits, in which the tom's ringing either stops out of nowhere, or there is a little "glitch" at the end of the hits. Now listen to the second segment of TRACK 59, which features the gate settings shown in Figure 75:

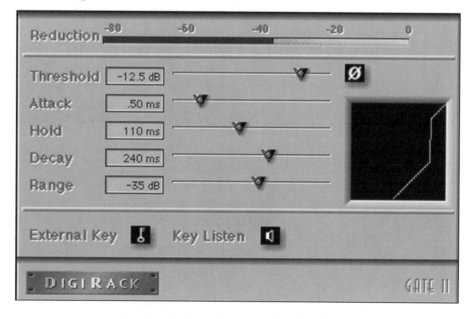

Fig. 75 – Settings for Track 59: TOM1 gate

We're still not finished yet. First, remember that I'll have to refine each tom sound individually before they will all sound good together. Right now, they are out of balance because TOM1 is the only tom accented so far. Plus, I've yet to apply some EQ, compression, and a bit of reverb. Figure 76 shows the settings for TOM1's EQ:

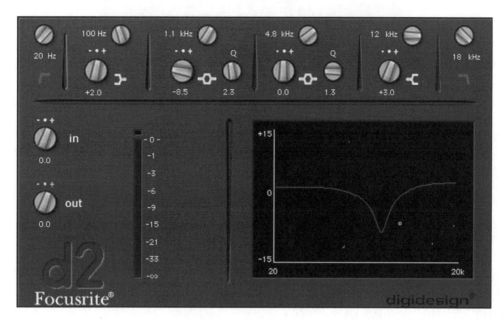

Fig. 76 – Settings for Track 60: TOM1 EQ

Since this tom track has been edited, I have more flexibility with the EQ settings. To "fatten up" the tom, I can add 100 Hz. I cut 1.1 KHz to remove some of the tom's "liveness," as I'll get enough "live" sound from the overheads and rooms.

NOTE: Some people prefer the drums to sound "live," and for them, I would recommend leaving in the 1 KHz frequency that I cut out. I prefer clean-sounding drums that fit into the mix wherever I want to insert them, as well as a lesser "live" sound, but not so much less that the result is a drum machine-type sound.

I also added 12 KHz in order to increase the stick sound and add clarity to the tom. If I had chosen a high-mid frequency, like 4–7 KHz, I would have been adding attack and harshness to the toms.

NOTE: The toms I'm using here have clear heads, but some drummers prefer the sound of batter heads, which tend to sound softer. In this case, adding some high mids will increase the "smack" of the toms.

Figure 77 shows the compressor settings, which will focus the sound and add an inoffensive "punch":

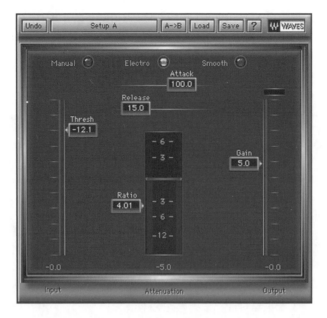

Fig. 77 – Settings for Track 60: TOM1 compression

Listen to TOM1 in the TRACK 60's mix now, panned at 10 o'clock. I've sent it to the same room reverb that I used for the kick and snare. The end of the groove still sounds edited, but that's only because I've not yet finished the other toms.

The kick, snare, and TOM1 now sound similar. TOM2 and TOM3 need some work now.

Tom2 and Tom3

We now have tracks with two more toms, TOM2 and TOM3, which I will edit similarly to that of TOM1. I will also use EQ, compression, and gating in order to achieve the sound I want. My objective is to try to make the toms stand out equally with the kick and snare. Figure 78 shows TOM2's EQ settings:

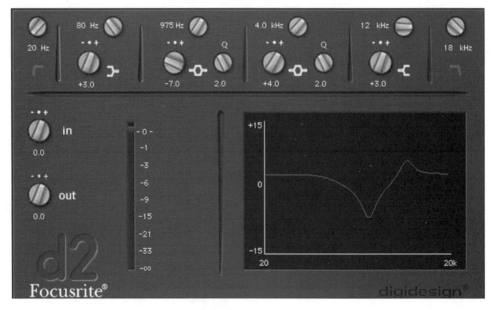

Fig. 78 – Settings for Track 61: TOM2 EQ

Figure 79 shows TOM3's EQ settings:

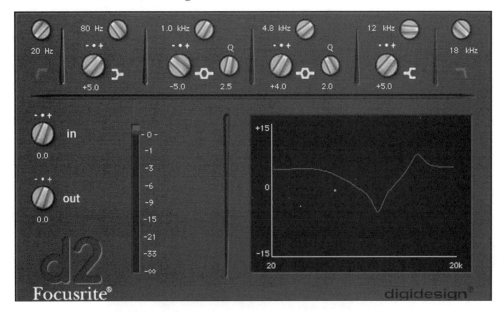

Fig. 79 – Settings for Track 61: TOM3 EQ

Figure 80 shows the compression settings for TOM2:

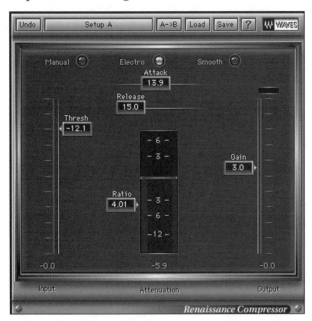

Fig. 80 – Settings for Track 61: TOM2 compression

Figure 81 shows the compression settings for TOM3:

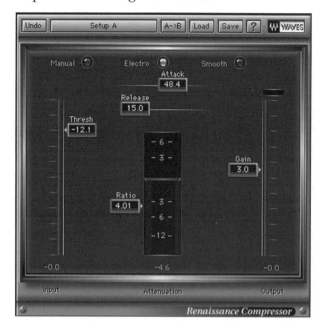

Fig. 81 – Settings for Track 61: TOM3 compression

Since I don't want my editing of the toms to sound obvious, I'll be using a gate as well. I should mention that I could avoid using a gate by putting fades on all the edited regions of my multitrack session. However, there is some bleed from the other toms inside these tracks, and the gate nicely reduces this bleed without being harsh. If you are a fan of fades, feel free to go that route. The important thing here is to be able to hear when either gates or fades are necessary.

Finally, I will add reverb similarly to that which I used on the kick, snare, and TOM1, so that they all sound as though they were recorded in the same room. I will also pan from the drummer's perspective, with the toms going from left to right. The final result can be heard on TRACK 61.

Hi-Hat

Last but not least is the hi-hat. This component does not figure into the groove, but is used during the beginning fill in order to keep time. Normally, I treat the hi-hat as an overhead, so I will need to roll off all low frequencies that do not affect it directly. Nor do I want a lot of bleed from the hi-hat when it is not being played. Therefore, for this groove, I will edit out all sections in which the hi-hat is not played. But for other grooves in which the hi-hat keeps time throughout, I would not edit it, but just roll off the unwanted frequencies instead.

NOTE: The hi-hat in these examples was played with the foot pedal only and was not actually being struck. It is important to be familiar with the different hi-hat sounds: open pedal, closed pedal, open hit, and closed hit. Make sure that you record each to sound as it should and the way that the drummer intended.

Just as I brought back the ghost notes from the bottom snare, I now want to bring the pedal hats back into the mix. To do this, I'm going to roll off 300 Hz and below, but otherwise leave the EQ alone. Then I'm going to add enough reverb to prevent it from sticking out too much when I do bring it up. Next, I'm just going to blend it in until it sounds like it fits. I usually bring it all the way out, then bring it up too loud, then back down all the way, and then slowly bring it up to where I feel comfortable with it. By doing it this way, I hear both extremes and can then find a happy middle ground. The hat will also be panned to the left, in order to maintain the integrity of the stereo mix we have created so far. Listen to TRACK 62, which now has the hat mixed in.

Take a look at Figure 82, which shows the fader level and panning of the sounds for TRACK 62. This should give you an idea of how to get the balanced sound heard on this track

Fig. 82 – Settings for Track 62: fader level and panning

Recording Musical and Playing Styles

In the following sections, I discuss the importance of musical and playing styles with regards to recording drums. What follows is a section on the kick drum sounds appropriate and customary to a few select musical styles, and the processing options available for obtaining the best possible of those sounds. We'll also look at the playing styles for snare drum and the sounds and processing appropriate to them.

Musical Styles and the Kick Drum

Blues-Shuffle Kick Sounds

Our first example is of a blues-shuffle drum part. We will start with a track captured with only two basic room microphones first. Listen to TRACK 63.

Where in this mix is the kick drum? Notice how soft it is? That's because it's customary for the drummer to play the kick a bit lighter for this style of beat. Therefore, to increase its volume a bit, I am going to place a D12 microphone just inside the kick. This now isolates and gives me control over the level of the kick. (Okay, that's not entirely true yet—I'll still have some bleed to deal with, but once I show you how to get rid of that, we will truly have full control over the accent level.) Now the resultant level of the kick will be dependant on two things:

1. The style/production of the song
2. The level of the bass guitar

The kick drum is usually supported and balanced by the bass guitar, meaning that their levels are pretty much even. But since the interaction and symbiosis of these two instruments is another subject entirely, I'm just going to point out for now that a good starting level for the kick is an even level with the snare. Listen to TRACK 64, which features the kick blended in just enough to balance out the level of the snare drum. The room sounds are panned left to right, and the kick is panned in the center.

Getting back to the style of the song: I have now listened to my "blues drums" reference CD, and after comparing my track to it, noticed that all of my sounds should to be much thinner—the basic/room sound should be smaller, and the kick should feature mostly the beater hitting the head with very little resonance.

In order to obtain the sound heard on my reference CD, I am going to apply the EQ settings shown in Figure 83 to my basic drum/room sound:

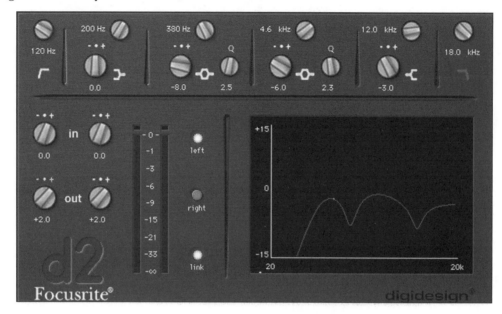

Fig. 83 – Settings for Track 65: EQ for basic drum/room sound

The 120 Hz roll-off on the bottom will take away all of the low overtones. Taking out 380 Hz will remove resonance and the woofy frequencies. I've also removed around 5 KHz to smooth out the attack on the cymbals.

Now the kick drum needs to be equalized as well. Figure 84 shows the settings:

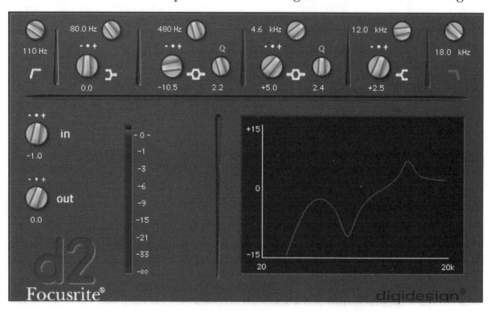

Fig. 84 – Settings for Track 65: EQ for kick

Here, I've thinned out the kick drum overtones as well, but added some attack by boosting around 5 KHz, and also added some clarity by boosting 12 KHz as well. Now listen to TRACK 65, which more closely represents the drum sounds that are on my "blues drums" reference CD. (You, too, should be trying to match your own tracks to a professional recording in the same style/genre.)

Let's now try a heavier drum sound.

Metal / Double Kick Sounds

This style incorporates a completely different kick sound than does blues. The kick—or double kick—is played fast. Therefore, there's no time for the kick sound to ring out and sustain, so the attacks need to be accurate, clear, and punchy. We're not looking for a "round" kick sound here at all. To capture this sound, I'm going to place the mic as far inside the drum as possible, and aim it directly at the beater. I'm also going to choose my punchy-sounding microphone: the 421. These two factors—mic choice and placement—eliminate half the battle of getting a tight, punchy kick sound to begin with.

Listen to TRACK 66, which again features just the basic/room mics. From this, I will remove some of the mud, or woofy frequencies, from the overall sound.

Do you notice how the kick drum needs to stand out a bit more? To remedy this, I'm going to blend in an accent microphone. But before I do, I'm going prepare the track by adding some EQ to the sound. Listen to the first segment of TRACK 67, which is the dry, pre-EQ sound captured by the 421 placed inside the kick. This actually sounds fine on it's own, but it's going to get a bit muddy when we blend it with the basic room sounds. Now listen to the second segment of TRACK 67. This is the 421 with the EQ settings shown in Figure 85:

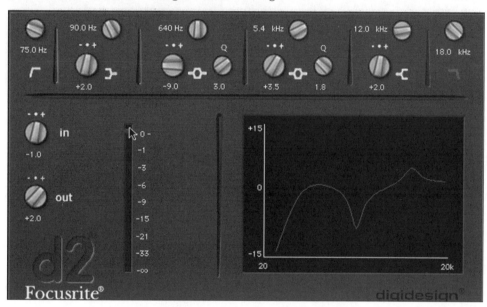

Fig. 85 – Settings for Track 67: EQ

This time, I removed the muddy frequencies a bit higher up (640 Hz); I didn't want the kick to be too thin, so I chose to leave 350 Hz alone and scoop it out higher. I added a little 5 KHz for the attack and 12 KHz for clarity. But only a little; otherwise it becomes too piercing and thin.

Now let's listen to the blend captured by all three microphones, with their processing, as heard on TRACK 68.

Hard / Heavy Rock Kick Sounds

The sounds for the double bass used in hard and heavy rock will only work for fast kick drum patterns. When the style is heavy, but the kicks far apart, the sound will need to be adapted accordingly. Listen to the first segment of TRACK 69, which is the basic drum/room sounds (with the same EQ settings as in Figure 24) played with a rock groove. Then listen to the second segment of TRACK 69, which features the dry (unprocessed) sound captured by the accent drum mic (the 421).

After comparing this track to my "heavy kick drum" reference CD, I realize that I need to add both EQ and compression to the kick sound. The compression will tighten up the punch even further. I'll use a 5:1 ratio, with a 100 ms attack, and 30 ms release. I'll also use about 3 dB of compression on each kick. Hear this on TRACK 70.

Figure 86 shows these EQ settings:

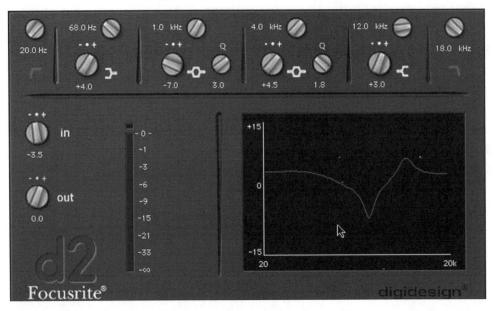

Fig. 86 – Settings for Track 70: EQ

I'm going to use compression after the EQ so that the peaks tighten up and don't distort at the output. The kick has attack, but is very short and punchy. Shifting and removing midrange frequencies up to 1 KHz allows the kick to retain more low-end, but not be as thin as it was in the example for double bass. In heavy rock, the kick is usually very solid, but also very short and clean. Let's hear the difference that all of this processing has made. The first segment of TRACK 71 features the dry basic/room sounds and the dry kick. Notice how round it sounds—not at all appropriate for hard/heavy rock. Now listen to the second segment of TRACK 71. This features all the processing mentioned above. Notice that now the kick sound is heavier and more aggressive, just like it should be.

Classic Rock / Huge Kick Sounds

Without mentioning the name, there was a classic rock band whose records were famous for their drum sounds. In particular, their kick drum sound, which was huge, has inspired many rock drummers since.

In order for you to create this huge kick sound, place a condenser microphone outside the kick drum. If you haven't skipped over the previous chapters, you'll remember that this placement will make the drum sound more open. Listen to the first segment of TRACK 72, which is the sound captured with the mic placed one foot outside the kick drum.

In order to increase the size and sustain of this kick, I'm going to add compression according to the settings shown in Figure 87:

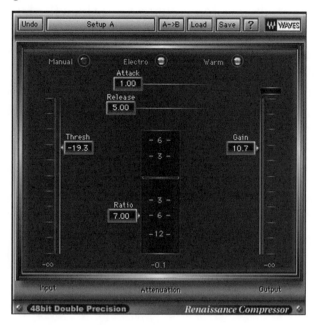

Fig. 87 – Settings for Track 72: compression

This compression will cause the kick drum to sound as it does on the second segment of TRACK 72. Notice how all of the attack has been removed, but the sustain has been massively increased.

All that is left now is to add the EQ settings as shown in Figure 88:

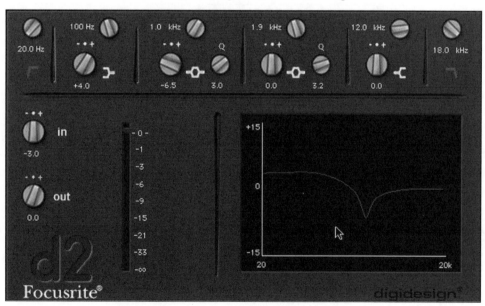

Fig. 88 – Settings for Track 72: EQ

Adding the 100 Hz of EQ will give back some of the body that had been squashed by the compressor. And removing around 1 KHz will reduce some of the bleed from the room, without compromising the kick. The third segment of TRACK 72 features the EQ and compression together.

Now let's put the processed accent tracks together with the basic drum/room sounds. Listen to the first segment of TRACK 73. We've used no reverb on this kick; this is just our natural sound changed by the overtones from the EQ and compression. Since the kick lacks some bite, I can add a microphone like the 421 placed close inside. The second segment of TRACK 73 features the 421 sounds blended in just enough to add some attack to the front of the kick notes.

Since we're on the subject of huge kick drums, maybe what you're looking for is a big reverb sound. Because you've probably recorded your drums in a modest-sized room, we can only increase the natural overtones so much. (And remember that, before we start adding effects to the accent mics' sounds, we need to clean up these tracks first.)

Adding Reverb to the Kick

Now let's move on to the reverb example. We're trying to get that huge kick drum sound, without having a huge room to record it in. Also, it's just the kick drum that we're trying to get big and boomy—not the whole drum kit. Listen to the first segment of TRACK 74, which features the edited kick drum track with the addition of "concert-hall" reverb. I then blended this with the room microphones. Notice how the kick is still "clean"; it's not all muddy and lost, but has a big ambience to it.

NOTE: Because I now have control over the kick resonance, I can use reverb to simulate different recording "spaces," like different-sized rooms, halls, or arenas. Your choices here depend on your reverb unit and how natural it sounds. As I mentioned above, I used a "simulation" reverb of an actual concert hall. But unlike the other processing settings I've used in this book, I have no illustrations of this simulation reverb to show or explain to you. That's because I just auditioned different reverb samples and chose this particular one. Most artificial reverbs will have several sample types to choose from, like room, hall, plate, chamber, spring, etc. As far as the kick drum goes, I made a choice between two types: "halls," which we just heard, and "rooms," which I would use for big, bombastic kicks.

However, if you want something a bit more natural and controllable than the concert-hall reverb of this track, go with a room reverb. The room reverb lets you simulate a room sound different from the one you actually recorded in. Let's listen to the second segment of TRACK 74, which features that same drum groove, but with a more natural, room reverb. I also mixed it a little louder than I normally would, so that you can hear it enough to compare it to the concert-hall reverb of the first segment.

The reverb you choose will be a matter of preference, but also a way to handle the short sounds that editing creates.

Playing Styles and the Snare Drum

Unlike the kick drum, which is always played with a beater head, the snare is played a number of different ways, and therefore produces a greater variety of tones.

Playing With or Without the Rim

Most drummers will play the snare by striking the drumhead and the rim simultaneously—but not always! The first segment of TRACK 75 features a snare hit on the head and rim together; the second segment features the head hits only. Notice the absence of the "crack" sound when the rim is not hit.

Playing Without the "Snare"

The "snare" is, technically, the metal chain-belt attached along the inner bottom-side of the drum. It's what gives the snare drum its "rattle" sound. Sometimes drummers will play with the metal snare released from the snare drum. It is also sometimes used as a substitute for a tom (if the snare is just too harsh), or with special wicker-like sticks to create different snare groove. TRACK 76 features an SM57 placed on a snare without its metal snare engaged.

Playing Sidestick

A playing style most popular in ballads, sidestick occurs when the drummer plays across the snare by cupping the stick in the palm. Sidestick is ideal for quiet song sections in which a loud snare, or even a softly-struck snare, is inappropriate. TRACK 77 features an example of this unique playing style, recorded unprocessed.

Recording Entire Drum Grooves

This section will take you through three drum groove styles, from their basic/room mic setups to their finished mixes. I will provide all the settings for the EQ, compression, gating, and/or other effects used, as well as mixing images that depict your levels and panning patterns. In addition to any processing, putting the final grooves together may also take some editing and possibly even some sound replacement. Use this section as your step-by-step guide for transforming your basic/room sounds into finished products. Take special notice of the settings, steps, or concepts that are consistently featured within the different styles, as these are the things that you can always rely on to improve the quality of your sounds.

Drum Groove Style 1: Metal

The original metal drum groove, without any processing or editing, can be heard on the first segment of TRACK 78. Now listen to TRACK 78's second segment, which is the finished product, complete with processing and editing. Follow along to learn how I got from A to Z.

I began by using the following mics, which I placed as indicated:

Kick Drum:

- Sennheiser 421 (dynamic), close to the beater head
- Rode NTK (condenser), 1' outside the kick drum hole

Snare Drum:

- Shure SM57 (dynamic) on top, 45-degree angle, 3" from rim
- AKG 451 (condenser) underneath, 45-degree angle, 10 dB pad, 6" away

Hi Hat:

- Neumann KM184 (condenser), 110-degree angle away from snare, 4" above hi-hat

Toms 1 & 2:

- Sennheiser 421 (dynamic), 60-degree angle, 3" from rim

Overheads:

- Two Shure KSM32 (condensers), spaced-pair setup, 3' above the cymbals

Rooms:

- Two Audix SCX25 (condensers), stereo image 20' apart, 20' from drum kit

The type of mic used—condenser or dynamic—is more important than which brand, but I've included that information for your reference. The goal here is to hear and understand how to accomplish the transformation of the original sounds into bigger, punchier, cleaner tones, which are most appropriate for this style of drumming.

Figure 89 shows the level and panning settings used:

Fig. 89 – Settings for Track 78: levels and panning

The Master 1 fader is used to control the overall output for the mixdown of the tracks onto a stereo format (CD).

The metal style of music calls for a tight double kick sound and a snare that cuts through the mix. Because the drummer had both feet occupied with the double kick pedal (on one kick drum, hence the double kick sound), the hi-hat, placed on the kit's right side, was played with a stick.

Listen to the first segment of TRACK 79 to hear our mix so far. The dry sounds are muddy and floppy, although they do sound "natural." But after listening to a "metal drum" reference CD, it was obvious that a "natural" drum sound was not appropriate for this groove.

The following sections break down the sound transformation per recording component:

Basic / Room Mics

You've already heard the first segment of TRACK 79, which is the room mics recorded dry. I decided that I needed to tighten up these sounds and remove the overtones causing muddiness. Figure 90 shows the EQ settings used to get the sound heard on the second segment of TRACK 79:

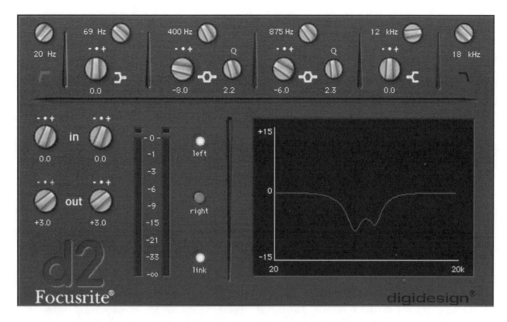

Fig. 90 – Settings for Track 79: EQ

It almost sounds here like I boosted the upper-mids and highs; but as you can see from Figure 90's settings, I did not. This is very important. If I had chosen to boost the upper-mids in order to clean things up, the sound would have instantly become harsh—especially when I got to the next step, which is compression.

Figure 91 shows the compression settings I used to bring up all the lost volume on the EQ. Listen to TRACK 80 to hear the result of this alteration.

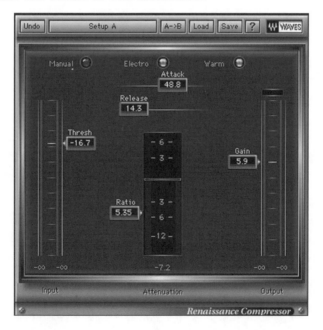

Fig. 91 – Settings for Track 80: compression

I am now getting closer to obtaining a tight, clean, and punchy drum sound.

Kick

The first segment of TRACK 81 features the kick drum tracks prior to editing. The second segment of TRACK 81 is the same track after a Pro Tools edit to remove any unnecessary bleed. I realize that this sounds a little weird, but hang in there with me. Once this track is blended with the room sounds, they sound like TRACK 82.

I was not happy with the abrupt endings that resulted from the edit, so I put the gate settings shown in Figures 92 and 93 on the kicks (recorded with the NTK and 421) as well:

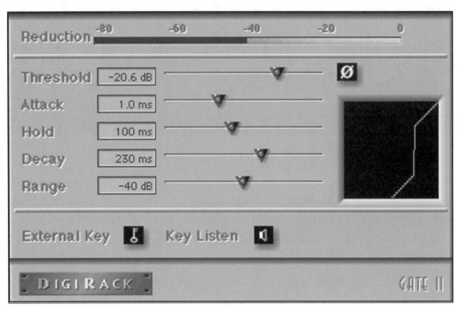

Fig. 92 – Settings for Track 83: gate for NTK (condenser)

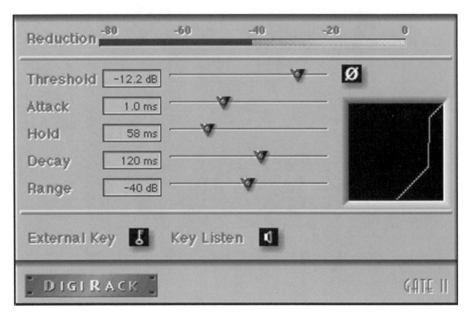

Fig. 93 – Settings for Track 83: gate for 421 (dynamic)

NOTE: In case you're wondering why I used both types of mics on the kicks: I wanted the dynamic to capture the sounds that were very sharp and quick-sounding, and the condenser to get the round, smooth, but also short sounds. When it comes to double bass, there isn't much room for fat or muddy sounds; otherwise, when the rest of the music gets mixed in, the drums will be lost in their own mud bath. Nor did I want the kick to get thin; so I used these two different sounds and blended them together to get the kick sound I was going for.

We still have some processing to do. Figures 94 and 95 show the EQ settings I used for the condenser and dynamic mics, respectively:

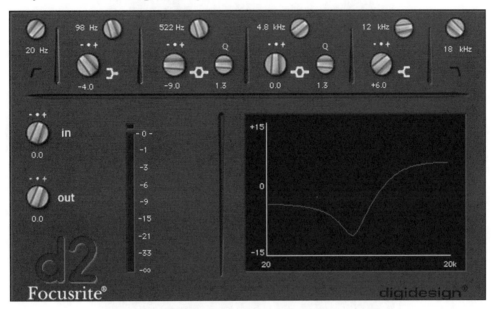

Fig. 94 – Settings for Track 83: EQ for NTK (condenser)

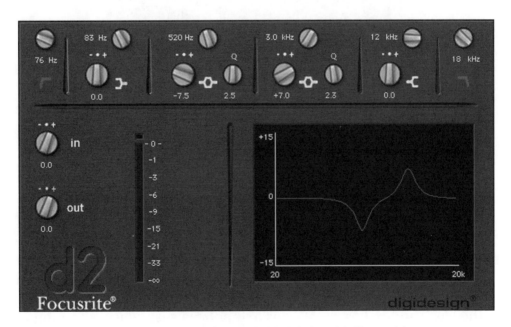

Fig. 95 – Settings for Track 83: EQ for 421 (dynamic)

Last but not least, I boosted and added punch to the kicks with the compression settings for each mic as shown in Figures 96 and 97:

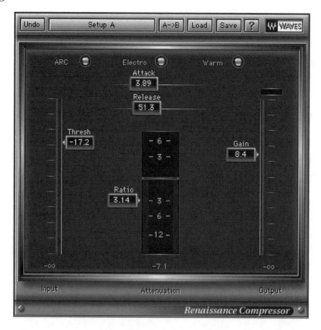

Fig. 96 – Settings for Track 83: compression for NTK (condenser)

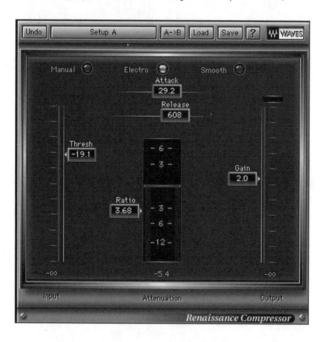

Fig. 97 – Settings for Track 83: compression for 421 (dynamic)

The result can be heard on TRACK 83. My main objective in adjusting the EQ and compression was to get a tight kick that wasn't too thin. However, on the kick's attacks, I continued to hear a little flamming (not tight attacks). I knew that this *flamming* was not due to the drummer's playing, so I looked at the kick's and rooms' waveforms and noticed that, when matching up their peaks, the rooms were slightly later than the kicks. This is natural, since the room microphones are 20' away from the kick, and the accent mics are extremely close to it. I decided to clean up the tracks by shifting, or nudging, the rooms to sound earlier, in order to match up their peaks with those of the kick's. (Shifting or nudging is another secret for tightening up sounds and removing unwanted discrepancies in your mixes.) So, after nudging my rooms backwards by about two-tenths of a second, the flams disappeared.

Snare

I wanted bring the snare out to the front of the mix and make sure that it had a nice "crack." I used the faders to blend the dry top and bottom sounds until I accomplished the sound heard on the first segment of TRACK 84. After that, I decided to edit the bottom snare, cut out all of the other sounds that were bleeding into it, and then put the gate settings shown in Figures 98 and 99 on the top and bottom snares, respectively:

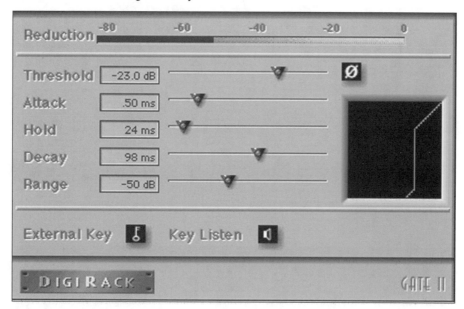

Fig. 98 – Settings for Track 84: gate for top snare

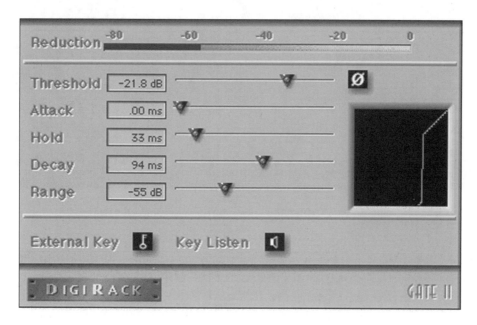

Fig. 99 – Settings for Track 84: gate for bottom snare

The result is that heard on the second segment of TRACK 84. The reasons that I wanted them to sound as short as they do is because they needed to blend in with the room sounds, and I wanted them ready for the reverb I planned to add to them later.

I next added the EQ settings shown in Figures 100 and 101 to the top and bottom snares in order to bring up some mids and highs—which I needed in order to balance out the upper-mids that were being brought out by the rooms:

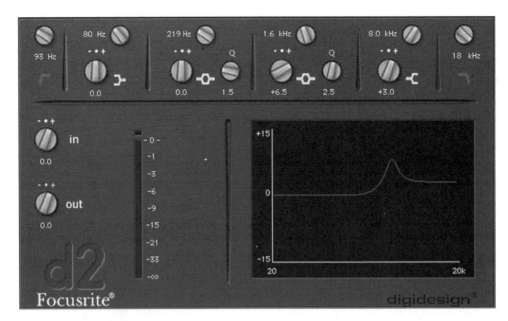

Fig. 100 – Settings for Track 85: EQ for top snare

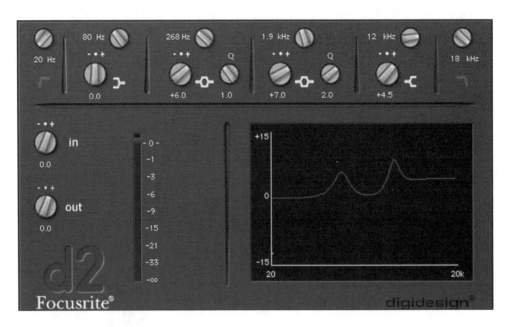

Fig. 101 – Settings for Track 85: EQ for bottom snare

Now we're ready for the compression that will tighten up the sound and make it "crack." This was another reason that I went for the mid instead of the upper-mid boost—I didn't want the crack to get too offensive when boosted, as upper-mids have a tendency to hurt when they get too loud. Figures 102 and 103 show the compression settings for the top and bottom snares, respectively:

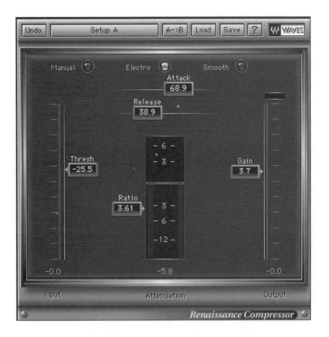

Fig. 102 – Settings for Track 85: compression for top snare

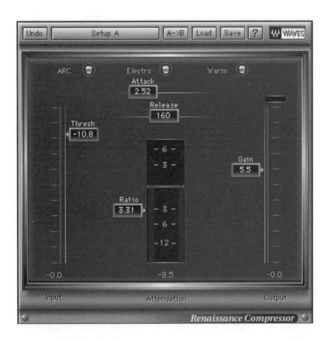

Fig. 103 – Settings for Track 85: compression for bottom snare

The two snare tracks now sound like the first segment of TRACK 85. I then blended that track in with the rooms and kicks to get the sounds heard on the second segment of TRACK 85.

Overheads

I decided to blend in the overheads before I blended in the hi-hat, because the cymbals need to be set at a certain level, and some of the hat will be in those sounds as well. (After I'm satisfied with the cymbal level, then I'll add whatever hat volume is necessary from the hi-hat track. This way, I'm not fighting with myself for different volumes from different tracks.)

The original overheads sounds can be heard on the first segment of TRACK 86. I realized that I needed to filter out as much of the other drum sounds as possible, because the rooms and the accent mics will pick up those sounds. So, I added the EQ filter settings shown in Figure 104:

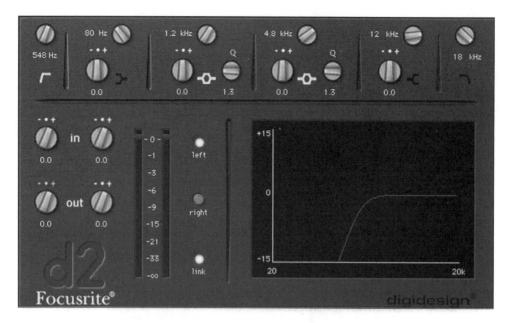

Fig. 104 – Settings for Track 86: EQ filter for overheads

That may seem like a lot of filtering, but since I'm going for clarity, I can remove even more low and low-mids than normal. Doing this made the whole track very clean, so I can now boost it with the compression settings shown in Figure 105:

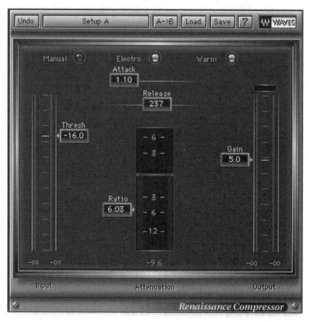

Fig. 105 – Settings for Track 86: compression for overheads

The compression actually has another purpose here, and that is to balance out the cymbals. Since I used the spaced-pair setup, and not XY, the volumes of the different cymbals will be a bit more dynamic than what I want to end up with; so these compression settings can therefore "even out" the cymbals to a more consistent volume. This will also keep the cymbals from sounding short and "patchy"; if the cymbals aren't compressed, the attack is heard, but the sustain is too soft to be heard over the other sounds, and so the cymbals just sound very sharp and short. Compression allows me to set the cymbal sound at a lower volume, while maintaining an overall sound that is consistently louder and therefore resonates longer.

Next, since metal drums require a more aggressive sound, I added the EQ settings shown in Figure 106:

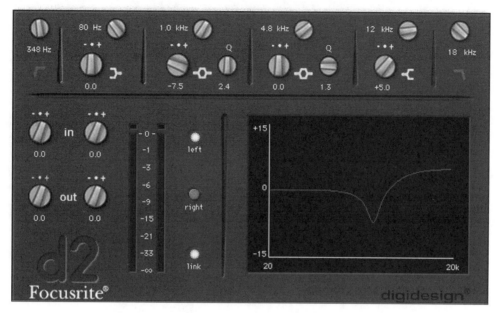

Fig. 106 – Settings for Track 86: EQ for overheads

The resultant overheads sound can be heard on the second segment of TRACK 86. Notice how they complement the overall drum sound. TRACK 87 features all the sounds we have together so far. A word of caution: it is extremely important not to over mix the overheads. Since the cymbals occupy most of the upper-mids and highs of the sound spectrum, they must be prevented from overshadowing the other drums; instead, they need to be blended in until they sit just behind the other drums.

Hi-Hat

In blending in the hi-hat, I wanted to be careful not to bring in any unwanted phasing or EQ problems. I noticed that the hi-hat wasn't being played in the beginning or end of the groove, but only in the middle; so I edited them. Normally, I wouldn't edit the hat track, but in this case it was necessary for clarity. Next, I filtered and equalized the track to remove any bleed from the other drums, and then compressed it to soften the attack just a little. While we could allow the other cymbals to be somewhat harsh, the hat needed to be a bit smoother in order blend in without itself becoming too harsh. Figures 107 and 108 show the settings for the EQ filter and the compression used:

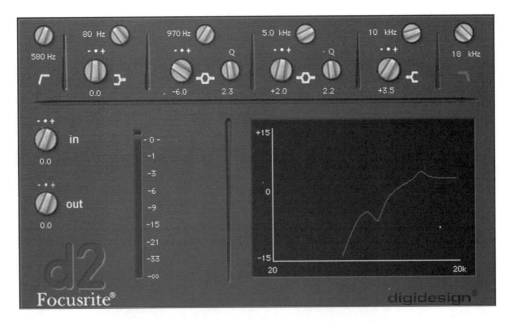

Fig. 107 – Settings for Track 88: EQ filter for hat

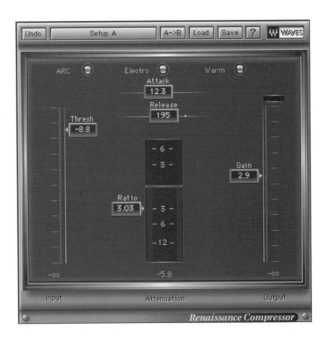

Fig. 108 – Settings for Track 88: compression for hat

So, what started as the dry track, which can be heard on the first segment of TRACK 88, became the processed sound heard on the second segment of TRACK 88. Blended in with everything thus far, we get TRACK 89.

Toms 1 & 2

That leaves only the toms. The toms are used as accents in this groove, and are only hit three times (TOM 2, TOM1, and TOM 2). Listen to the original tom tracks on TRACK 90. As you can hear, there is a lot of bleed from the other drum sounds. I decided to edit the tracks so that only the three hits remained on these tracks. I also noticed that the last hit (TOM2) was lighter than normal because the drummer was going past the toms pretty quickly. I decided to edit again, and replaced the last TOM2 hit with a copy of the first TOM2 hit. This gave me the best raw material to work with before applying EQ and compression.

On TOM1, I applied the EQ and compression settings shown in Figures 109 and 110:

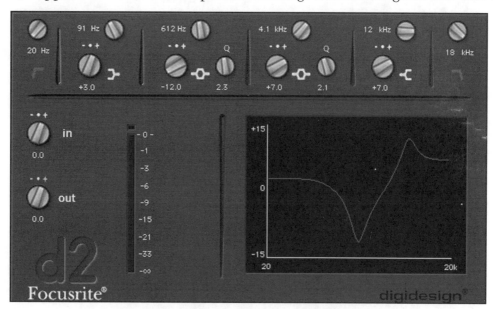

Fig. 109 – Settings for Track 91: EQ for TOM1

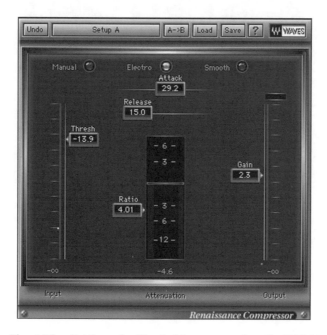

Fig. 110 – Settings for Track 91: compression for TOM1

After adding punch and clarity to TOM1, the edit was obvious, so I added a gate to hide the abrupt ending:

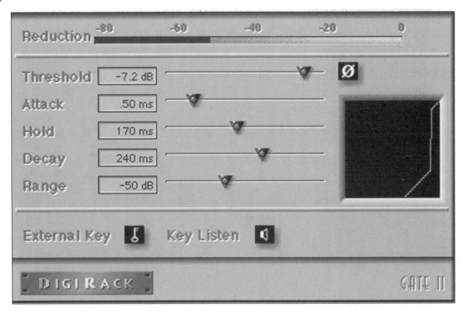

Fig. 111 – Settings for Track 91: gate for TOM1

I applied the same processing philosophy to TOM2, and used the EQ, compression, and gating settings shown in Figures 112–114:

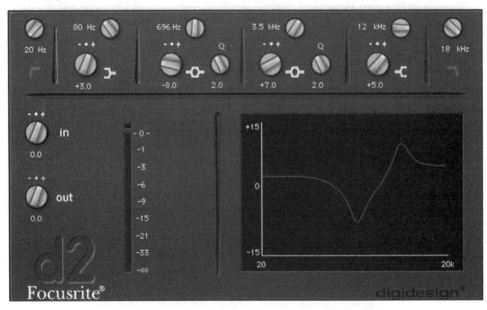

Fig. 112 – Settings for Track 91: EQ for TOM2

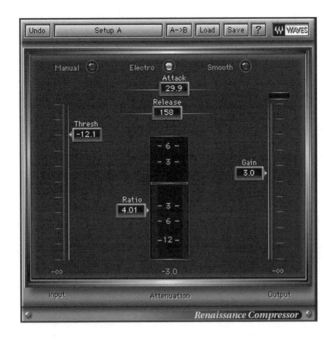

Fig. 113 – Settings for Track 91: compression for TOM2

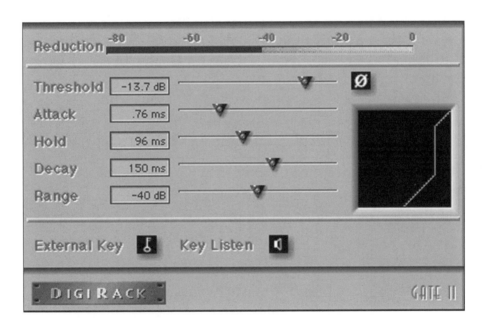

Fig. 114 – Settings for Track 91: gating for TOM2

The newly processed three hits can be heard on TRACK 91.

And putting it all together so far, we get TRACK 92.

Reverb and Master Fader Limiting

Okay, so with all of the editing and gating, I decided to give all of the sounds (except the 421 kick and rooms) a room reverb sound. This will increase the conceptual size of the performance and give it dimension. Last but not least, I put a limiter on the output of the master fader to maximize the volume that will be printed in stereo. As mentioned earlier in this book, a limiter is like a compressor, but is primarily used instead to keep a track from peaking by suppressing the peaks that would normally cause clipping and unwanted distortion. Since I did not intend for these tracks to be "mastered" by a mastering engineer, I needed to make sure that this transformed groove had the impact of a professional drum sound when completed. Therefore, I used a limiter to get a few extra decibels of volume without the noticeable effect of a compressor.

We now have our transformed groove, which you listened to when you began this chapter's section, from the second segment of TRACK 78. Listen to it again to also hear the reverb and master fader limiting changes done. And also notice again the huge difference between the dry tracks and the final, processed mix.

Drum Groove Style 2: Ballad

Now let's take a different direction with the drum sounds. Instead of short, punchy sounds with lots of attack, let's go for the big, open, and natural sound typical of ballads. Sometimes the term "natural" is ascribed to sounds that seem to have been recorded in someone's garage—that's not what I mean here. "Natural," in this case, means that there are overtones still present when each sound was created. The transformation of this ballad groove will be harder to accomplish than that of the metal drum groove; as each sound will need to be held for a longer period of time, we have to make sure that we get enough resonance.

I began by using the following mics, which I placed as indicated:

Kick Drum:

- AKG D112 (dynamic), just inside the outer head
- Rode NTK (condenser), 1' outside the kick drum hole

Snare Drum:

- Shure SM57 (dynamic), on top 45-degree angle, 3" from rim
- AKG 451 (condenser) underneath, 45-degree angle, 10 dB pad, 6" away

Hi Hat:

- Neumann KM184 (condenser), 110-degree angle away from snare, 4" above hats

Toms 1, 2, & 3:

- Sennheiser 421 (dynamic), 60-degree angle, 3" from rim

Overheads:

- Two Shure KSM32 (condensers), spaced-pair setup, 3' above the cymbals

Rooms:

- Two Audix SCX25 (condensers), stereo image 20' apart, 20' from drum kit

The only change from the metal drum setup is the kick microphone—I substituted the AKG D112 for the 421 and backed it away from the beater head. I could have still used the 421, but for the sake of this book, I thought it best to demonstrate for you an additional mic option. Also, the D112 has less attack than the 421, which will get me closer to the ballad sound I'm after.

To start, let's listen to TRACK 93, which features the dry, unprocessed basic sound. Figure 115 shows the levels and panning settings used:

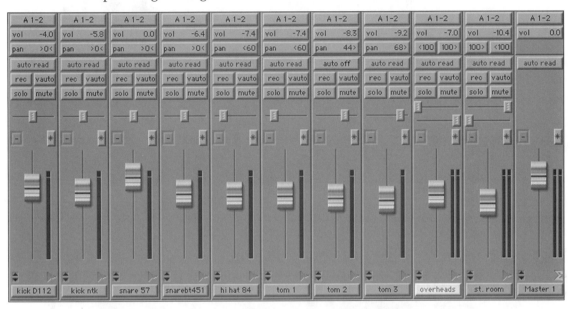

Fig. 115 – Settings for Track 93: levels and panning

The final mix of this groove transformation can be heard on TRACK 94.

In the following sections, I've broken down the drum kit by component to explain each step of the ballad transformation.

Kick

In creating the mic blend for the kick, I first edited out all of the unwanted bleed from the D112, so that the sound captured would be punchy without being harsh (kind of a "thud" sound). Next, because the editing got a little choppy-sounding, I added a gate for a smooth fade on each hit. Figure 116 shows these gate settings:

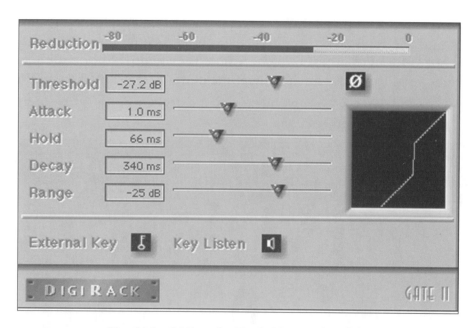

Fig. 116 – Settings for Track 95: gate for D112

Figure 117 shows the EQ settings:

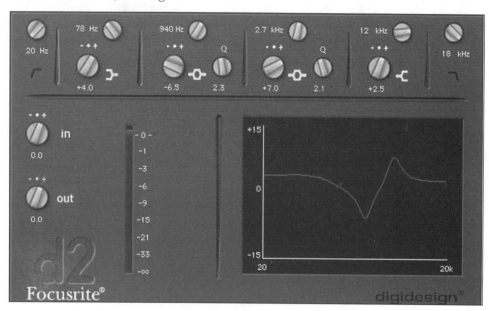

Fig. 117 – Settings for Track 95: EQ for D112

Finally, I added a bit of limiting, as shown in Figure 118, in order to increase the size and density of the kick:

Fig. 118 – Settings for Track 95: limiting for D112

Listen to the first segment of TRACK 95, which features the dry kick sound as originally recorded. The second segment of TRACK 95 features the same track after the editing and processing described above. Notice those elements that were changed or removed, all without ruining the sound of the original kick track.

The condenser microphone was placed outside the kick to capture as "live" a sound as possible without also picking up any unwanted bleed. I began here as well with editing. Figure 119 shows the track before this edit:

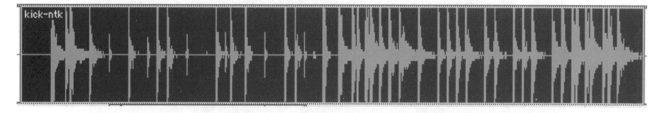

Fig. 119 – Settings for Track 96: before editing NTK

Figure 120 shows this track after removing the bleed from the other sounds:

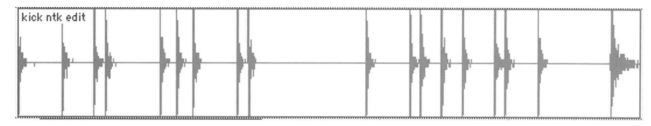

Fig. 120 – Settings for Track 96: after editing NTK

Figures 121–123 show the settings used for the gate, EQ, and limiter:

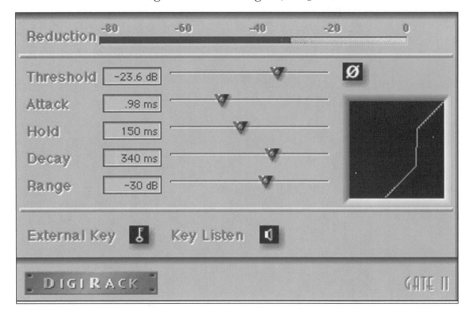

Fig. 121 – Settings for Track 96: gate for NTK

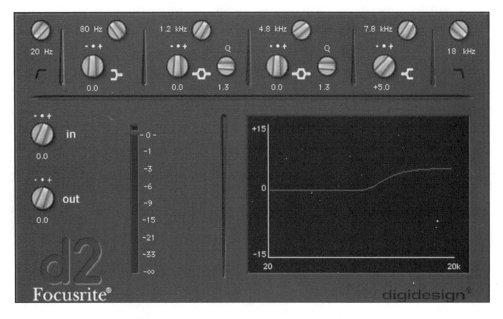

Fig. 122 – Settings for Track 96: EQ for NTK

Fig. 123 – Settings for Track 96: limiter for NTK

As I mentioned before, I wanted a very "live" feel for the kick, so I also used a room reverb in order to add some clean sustain to the sound. Doing so made it sound as if I placed the mic even further outside the kick, but without losing clarity or capturing bleed from the other sounds. The reverb also widened the kick, allowing it to fill up more space.

On both kick tracks, I also replaced "noisy" kicks with "quieter" kicks. When big cymbal crashes occur at the same time as the kick (such as what often happens on the "1" of a measure), the crashes bleed into the kick track, no matter what editing or gating was applied. To eliminate the noisy tracks, I copied one of the earlier, quieter kick tracks that had less (or no) bleed and replaced the noisy one with it. When doing this, you really have to pay attention to dynamics, however; you can't just grab any kick, otherwise you could ruin the relevant accents that the drummer played. I took care to find and choose a kick sound with equal intensity.

Listen to the first and second segments of TRACK 96, which feature the before and after sounds of the NTK placed outside the kick—first without processing, then with.

These sounds blended together very well, complementing each other instead of clashing.

Snare

I chose this particular groove because of its sidestick part. I thought it was a great example of how to deal with a snare track comprised of completely different sounds. So, to start, I duplicated the track and separated the sidestick parts from the full snare parts. Figures 124 and 125 show the snare tracks before and after editing, respectively.

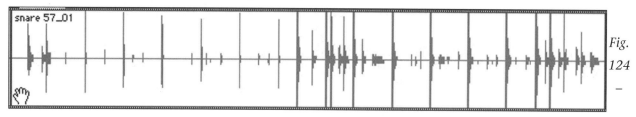

Fig. 124 –

Settings for Track 94: snare before editing

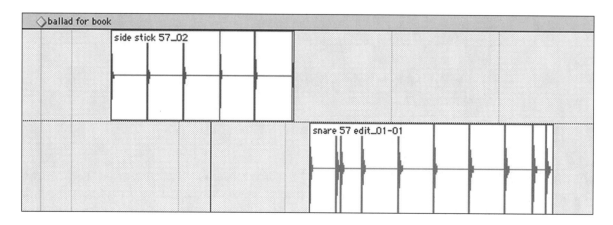

Fig. 125 – Settings for Track 94: snare after editing

Having done this editing, I can now apply different EQ, compression, reverb and gating settings without worrying about automating the changes. You may have noticed, if you'd looked closely enough at these two figures, that these tracks had also been edited to remove unwanted bleed.

Figure 126 shows the compression settings applied to the sidestick track:

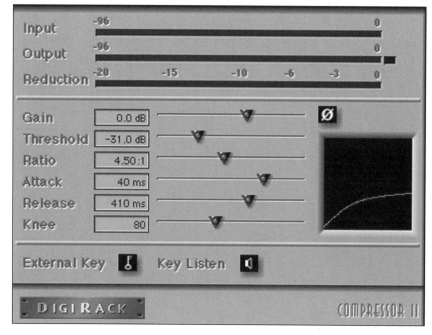

Fig. 126 – Settings for Track 94: sidestick compression

Figure 127 shows the EQ settings that were also applied to the sidestick tracks in order to get from it a brighter attack:

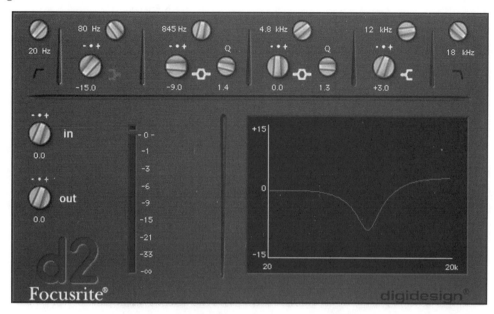

Fig. 127 – Settings for Track 94: sidestick EQ

I then decided to use a bright hall reverb; but because I didn't want it to sound too extreme, I added a bit of room reverb to it as well. The hall reverb was also used to create a longer sustain, and the room reverb helped to blend it with the overall drum sound.

I realized, however, that the room sounds were not blending well with this new sidestick sound. Altering the room sound was not an option, nor did I want to change the sidestick sound. What I chose to do was remove the room sound whenever the sidestick was playing. But I didn't want to remove the room sounds with an edit or a gate, so I chose instead to use a *sidechain*. To accomplish this, I placed a limiter on the rooms and triggered, or "keyed," them according to the sidestick. Every time the sidestick was hit, the limiter would activate and apply about 18 dB of compression, but only for as long as the sidestick lasted (which was only for an instant). So to sidechain, then, in this case, is to use a limiter to compress the rooms for the duration of the sidestick. (This may be a bit complicated for our purposes; don't worry if it doesn't make complete sense. I just found that the cleanest way to blend the room and the sidestick together was with the sidechain, and I wanted you to be aware of this useful option.)

Now on to the regular snare sound. The snare of choice for this type of groove is typically a nice wood snare, which will sound rounder and softer than other snares. Figures 128–130 show the settings that I applied to the top snare sound for the gate, EQ, and compressor:

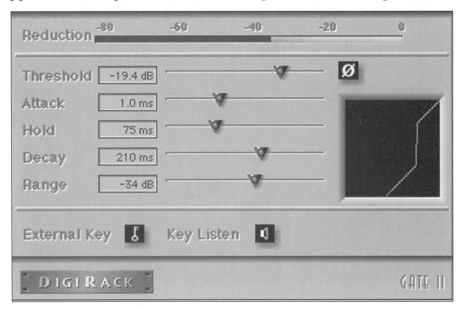

Fig. 128 – Settings for Track 94: top snare gate

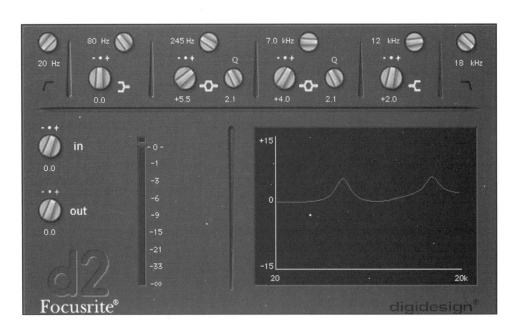

Fig. 129 – Settings for Track 94: top snare EQ

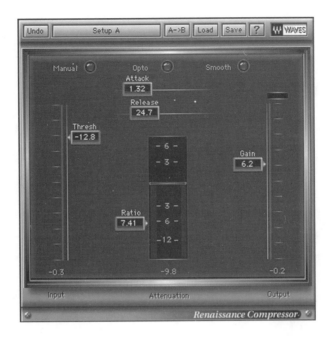

Fig. 130 – Settings for Track 94: top snare compression

And, as usual, I edited out all of the unwanted bleed from the track.

For the full snare sound, I purposely wanted a longer, bigger reverb, because I wanted it to be noticeable and to add a "trail" to the snare. I gained most of this reverb by sending the top snare sound to the reverb plug-in.

For the bottom snare, I wanted to avoid too much harshness, but retain most of the brightness. I edited the track again, but had to take care not to cut out the ghost notes in the second half of the groove. Figures 131–133 show the settings that I applied to the bottom snare for the gate, EQ, and compressor:

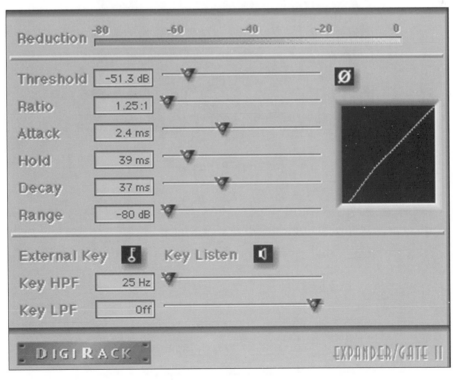

Fig. 131 – Settings for Track 94: bottom snare gate

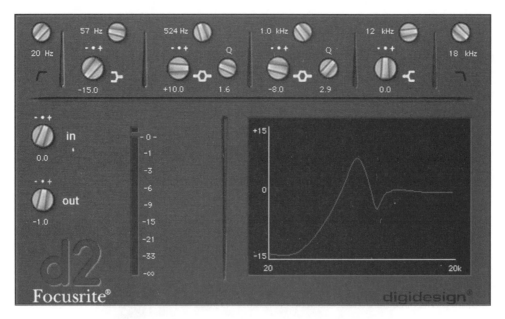

Fig. 132 – Settings for Track 94: bottom snare EQ

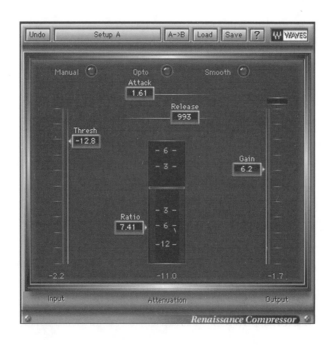

Fig. 133 – Settings for Track 94: bottom snare compression

I also made sure to add a little room reverb, plus a little of the longer hall reverb, so that both the top and bottom snares' sounds blended well together.

Listen once again to TRACK 94, to hear the final mix of this transformed groove.

Hi-Hat

Figure 134 shows the EQ settings for this hi-hat track: settings:

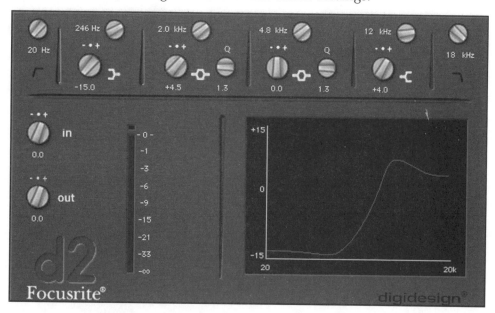

Fig. 134 – Settings for hi-hat: EQ

The EQ here acted mainly as a filter, in order to remove the other drum sounds from the hi-hat track. I also added a little high-end to keep it "sparkling."

Since the second half of the groove features the ride cymbal keeping time instead of the hats, the hat track also needed editing. And in order to create a smooth transition, I faded out the track. Figure 135 shows the fader settings used:

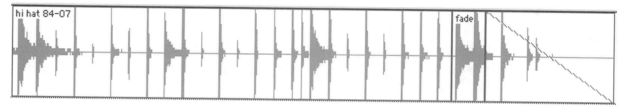

Fig. 135 – Settings for hi-hat: fader

Last but not least, I sent this track to the room reverb to give it a bit of ambience.

Toms 1, 2 & 3

Three toms were used for this groove. The first thing I did was edit out everything except the toms from the tracks. I did a little replacement here as well, particularly the track for TOM1, which included some noisy cymbal hits that could not be removed. I therefore just replaced the noisy hits with some of the same tom's quieter hits that occurred earlier in the track.

Other that the edit/replacement, the room reverb played the biggest role in capturing the toms' sounds. The reverb also helped keep the toms nice and big, but very clean. Figures 136–144 show the settings that I used for the gate, EQ, and compressor on TOMS1, 2, and 3, respectively:

TOM1

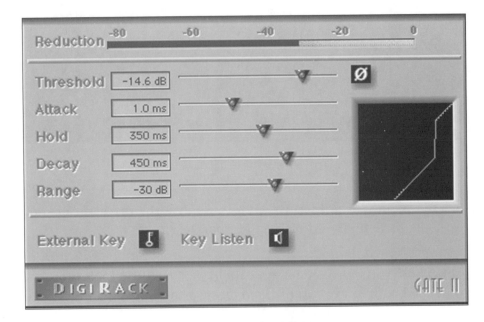

Fig. 136 – Settings for TOM1: gate

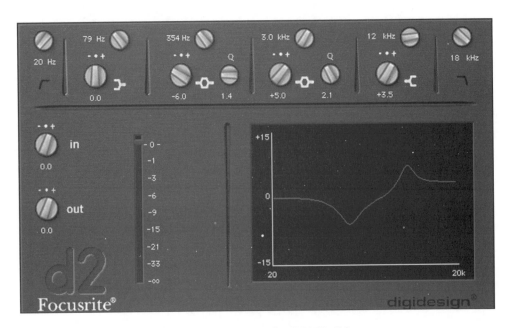

Fig. 137 – Settings for TOM1: EQ

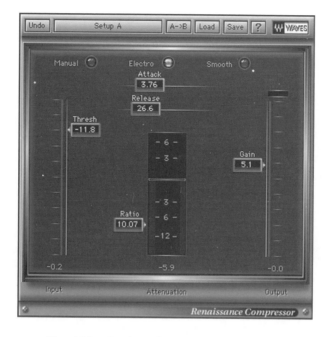

Fig. 138 – Settings for TOM1: compression

TOM2

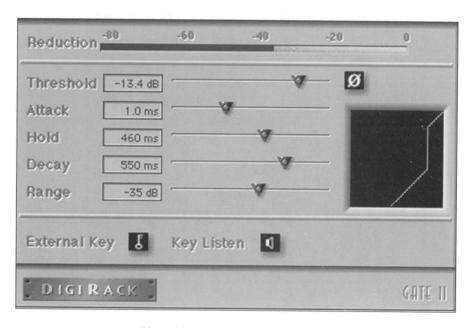

Fig. 139 – Settings for TOM2: gate

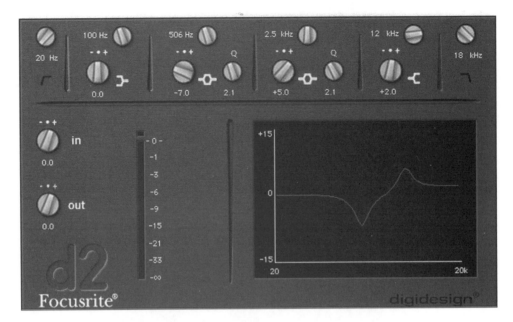

Fig. 140 Settings for TOM2: EQ

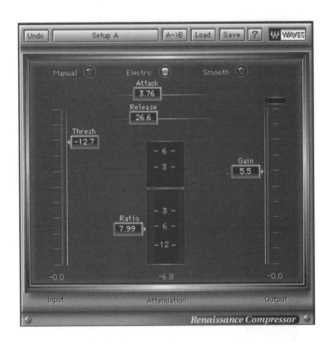

Fig. 141 – Settings for TOM2: compression

TOM3

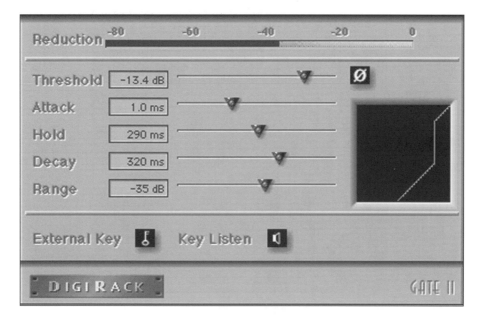

Fig. 142 – Settings for TOM3: gate

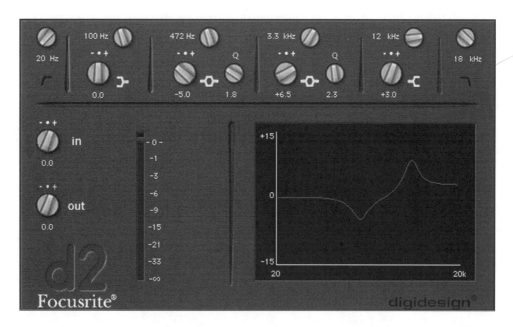

Fig. 143 – Settings for TOM3: EQ

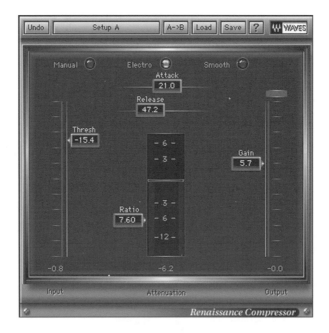

Fig. 144 – Settings for TOM3: compression

Of course, panning and levels were also crucial, and it took several listens before I was able to fine-tune them.

Overheads

Figures 145 and 146 show the EQ and compression settings for the overheads:

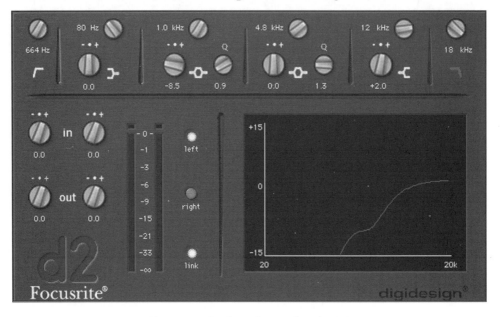

Fig. 145 – Settings for overheads: EQ

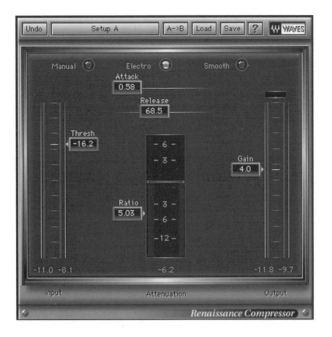

Fig 146 – Settings for overheads: compression

The overheads needed to capture the ride cymbals loudly enough to allow them to match the level of the hi-hat, so that the transition lost nothing. However, the crashes needed to be controlled so that they did not take up too much space. The volume of the crashes and ride were balanced with compression. The EQ was used here again mainly as a filter, but also to add some brilliance to the cymbals. And, in order to get these sounds to blend in with the rest of the track, I sent them to the room reverb.

Basic / Room Sounds

As for the original room sound, Figures 147 and 148 illustrate the settings used for the EQ and compressor:

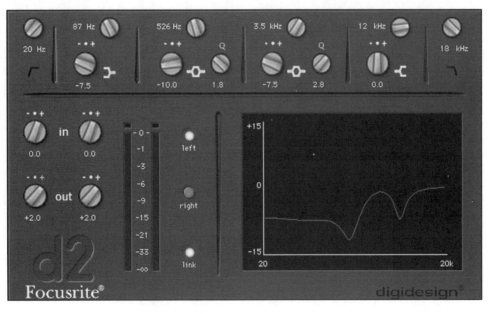

Fig. 147 – Settings for basic/room sound: EQ

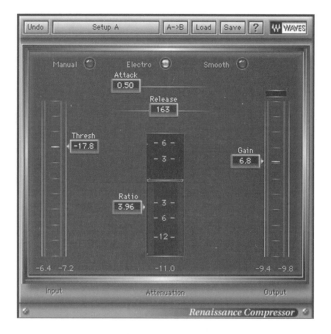

Fig. 148 – Settings for basic/room sound: compression

This track had to be shifted backwards slightly, in order line up the attacks with the snare and kick. Otherwise, I just used the EQ settings shown to clean up the rooms, and the compressor to soften the attacks to better fit this style of groove.

Reverb

I used two reverbs: one was a room reverb, in order to add depth, and the other was a hall reverb on the snare, in order to add length or a "trail." The snare reverb was not sounding exactly the way I wanted, so I added an EQ with the settings shown in Figure 149:

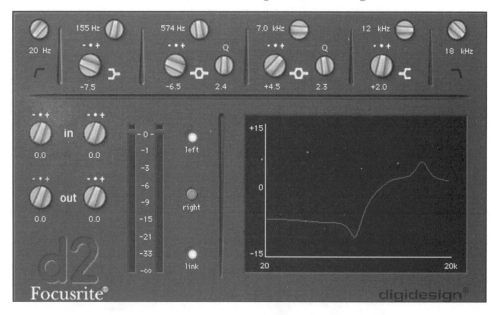

Fig. 149 – Settings for reverb EQ

Master Fader

I placed a limiter on the master fader, which allowed me to maximize the volume of the track without distortion. Because I only used 3 dB of limiting, its inclusion was inaudible.

Figures 149 and 150 illustrate what the final mix and edit looked like:

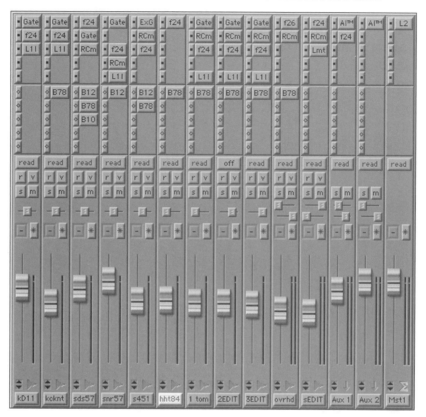

Fig. 149 – Settings for ballad final mix

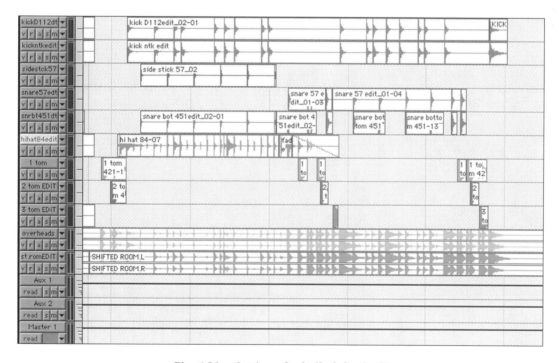

Fig. 150 – Settings for ballad final edit

Listen once again to the final mix on TRACK 94 to hear the full transformation of this groove.

Drum Groove Style 3: Tight Pop / Country

The objective of this example is to move away from a natural room sound and use the accent mics to create a tight, controlled sound. I will also be using reverb in order to add a controlled ambience to the overall sound. With a musical style like this, the sounds of the other instruments are often more vital to the mix than the sound of the drums. So here, I really just need to maintain the drums in this mix as element for keeping time. Whenever this is the case, I usually end up editing and gating like a fiend and sometimes even removing the room sounds entirely. For this mix, when all was said and done, the kick and snare came out as very distinct and blended well with the other instruments without getting lost.

The primary focus should be on getting clarity and definition from the kick and snare, and time-keeping from the hat or ride. If you try to throw in a bunch of room sounds, the mix will become muddy as the other instruments crowd the now-limited space.

I began by using the following mics, which I placed as indicated:

Kick Drum:

- AKG D12 (dynamic), well inside the drum

Snare Drum:

- Shure SM57 (dynamic), on top, 45-degree angle, 2" from rim
- AKG 451 (condenser) underneath, 45-degree angle, 4" from bottom

Hi Hat:

- Neumann KM184 (condenser), 110-degree angle away from snare, 4" above hats

Overheads:

- Two Shure KSM32 (condensers), spaced-pair setup, 3' above the cymbals

Rooms:

- Two Audix SCX25 (condensers), stereo image 20' apart, 20' from drum kit

TRACK 97 is an example of a "tight," "non-live-sounding," drum recording. The original tracks are featured on TRACK 98. Figure 151 shows the levels and panning settings for the tight mix:

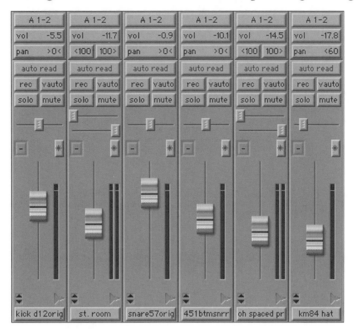

Fig. 151 – Settings for Track 97: final mix levels and panning

These kinds of settings work well when the drums' primary role is to keep time. Take a listen to a pop reference CD that was recorded with live drums, but doesn't sound like it was recorded with live drums. What you're hearing on such recordings is not a loop, a sample, or a drum machine, yet the sound has a more canned or mechanical quality. For this groove example, we will replicate such a sound.

Let's address each of the components used for getting this groove's style of drum sound.

Kick

Because a condenser would not capture a "tight" kick sound, I used the D12 (dynamic) placed well inside the drum. Also, because I needed a kick that did not fluctuate in dynamics (unless called for), I ended up cutting the noisy kick drum hits from this track, copying a couple of quieter hits from the same groove, and replacing the noisy hits with the quieter copies.

I also heavily compressed the kick so it would be very even-sounding and "thumpy." Figure 152 shows the compression:

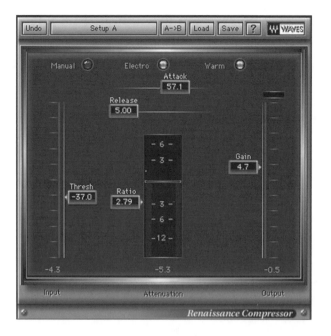

Fig. 152 – Settings for Track 97: compression for kick

Notice the short release time, which will keep the kick from getting over-compressed.

I also used the following EQ settings shown in Figure 153 in order to remove all of the kick's "live" sound:

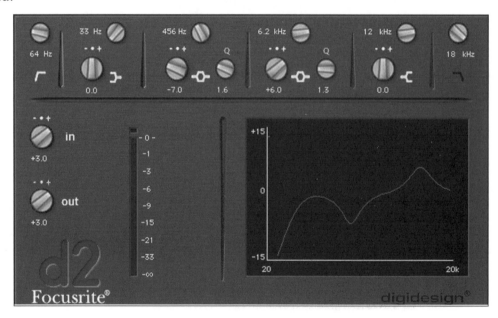

Fig. 153 – Settings for Track 97: EQ for kick

Nothing fancy here; and extra low-end is unnecessary.

Snare

The snare sound is an important element of this groove, as is its consistency. To capture the snare sound, I used an SM57, placed about 2" away from the top head. I ended up editing the snare and using only two actual, but different, hits, removing any bleed, and replacing all rest with these copies. The result is a snare that sounds extremely accurate. Again, I'm not worried about retaining any of the natural tonal changes that would normally occur in such a groove; I'm concerned about tracking a very consistent sound and controllable dynamic. Figures 154 and 155 show the EQ and compression settings used on this track:

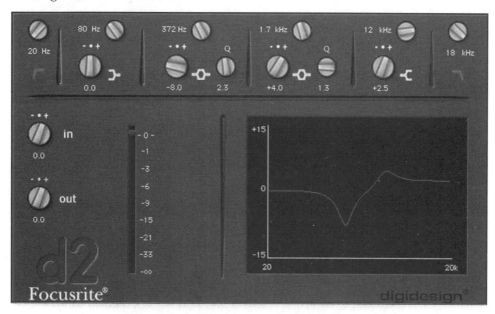

Fig. 154 – Settings for Track 97: top snare EQ

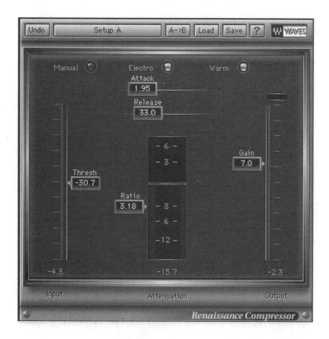

Fig. 155 – Settings for Track 97: top snare compression

The snare had a bit of undesirable "ring" to it, which was cleaned up by removing the low-mid frequencies. I also sent the snare to a natural room reverb to clean up the edits and create the illusion of room sound. Because the rooms get muddy naturally from the bleeding of other sounds, but the accent mics don't get muddy when fed to a nice reverb, this was the way to go. The reverbed track is clean, clear, and sounds like its whole kit was in a room.

Because of ghost notes, the bottom snare was crucial to this track. I used a condenser placed 4" beneath the bottom snare. I opted not to let the ghost notes be picked up by the top snare mic (I didn't like the sound I got from doing this) and chose to bring out the fills around the snare through the bottom. I edited, but did not replace any sounds, and just removed what I could when the snare wasn't being played. Figures 156–158 show the settings for the gate, EQ, and compressor for the bottom snare's tracks, which I also sent to the same reverb as the top snare's tracks.

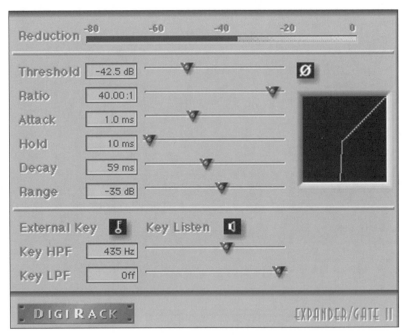

Fig. 156 – Settings for Track 97: bottom snare gate

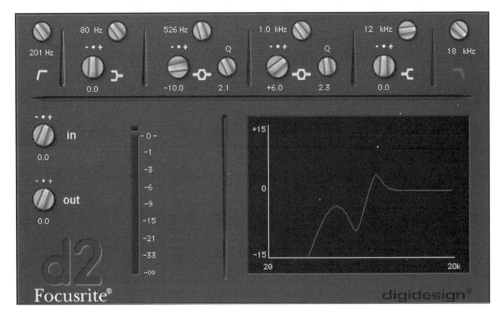

Fig. 157 – Settings for Track 97: bottom snare EQ

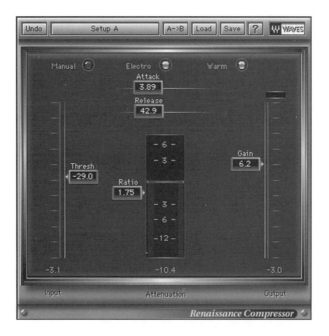

Fig. 158 – Settings for Track 97: bottom snare compression

Notice that the top snare consists of a short, "poppy" sound, while the bottom snare "rustles" without being harsh.

Hi-Hat

The hi-hat follows the same concepts conveyed in the previous grooves. I used a condenser (placed 4" away from the top hat), as well as EQ, compression, and a room reverb. The EQ here removes all the unwanted bleed from the other drums, while the compressor evens it out. Also very important here is to set a level that is not too loud or soft, and to pan it.

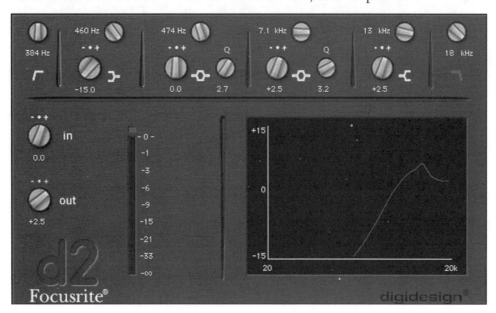

Fig. 159 – Settings for Track 97: hi-hat EQ

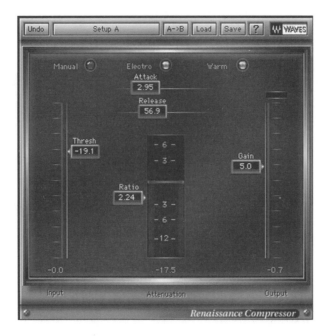

Fig. 160 – Settings for Track 97: hi-hat compression

Overheads

The ride cymbal is important to this groove, so I can't bury the cymbals. Since the crashes get out of hand when the level is too loud, we'll use EQ to remove unwanted bleed and compression to even it all out. This track was also sent to the room reverb for added ambience.

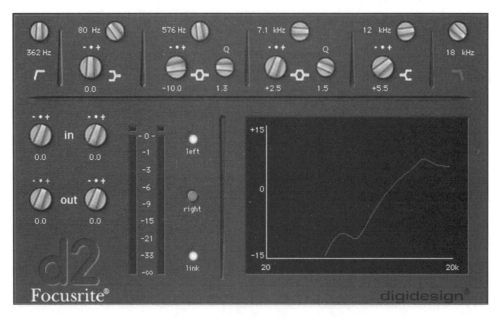

Fig. 161 – Settings for Track 97: overheads EQ

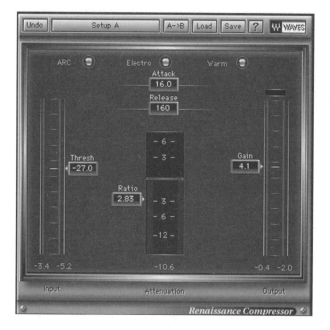

Fig. 162 – Settings for Track 97: overheads compression

Basic / Room Sounds

I chose to remove the room sounds completely, which helps when you just can't get a decent room sound out of your kit. Sometimes the rooms are just not needed.

Reverb

For this groove, I used just one nice room reverb that produced a clear and natural sound.

Master Fader

As I'd done on previous examples, I used a limiter on the output of the master fader in order to bring up all of the levels, while I mixed down, without peaking.

Listen again to the final transformed groove sound—the "tight" drum mix—as heard on TRACK 97.

Closing Note

So, there you have it. I realize that, for some of you, this book may not be an easy read filled with quick tricks and fix-its. I've spent a great deal of time on trial and error; I hope that some of what I've learned as a result will be of benefit to you. As you gain recording experience, I'm confident that the ideas, concepts, and techniques described throughout will become some of your most useful and essential tools.

The basic concept herein is to treat each drum individually, while remembering that each is part of a whole. Also, don't be afraid to try radical settings; innovation can be the key to a desired outcome. Listen to your reference drum sounds and try, at first, to imitate. Such is a kind of education that is often disregarded because of ego, pride, or ignorance.

I hope you enjoy recording drums even more, now that you have some ideas and tools for reaching your goals.

Dallan

Acknowledgements

- Drums performed amazingly by Jeff "Super Jeff" Bowders.
- Tracked at the Recording Institute at MI in Studio A.
- Tracked, edited, and mixed on Pro Tools HD by Dallan Beck.
- Mixed and edited at Karma Studios.
- Cover photography by Tevis Sauer Karlsson.

Special thanks to:
- The light of my life: Hila Calif
- The reason I pursued recording and music: TJ Helmerich.
- The reason I exist and live happily: my parents, Alice and John.
- The invaluable support and love of: Jennifer and Jim Hancock and Bob Skewis.
- Those who allowed my books to be a reality: Jeff Schroedl and everyone at Hal Leonard Corp.
- Those companies who granted permission for the use of the screen shots included herein: Digidesign (a division Avid Technology, Inc), Waves, and Audio Ease.

Illustration Credits

Screen shots used with permission and provided by:
- Digidesign (a division of Avid Technology, Inc.) ©2003
- Waves
- Audio Ease

Photographs used with permission and provided by:
- Tevis Sauer Karlsson

Musicians Institute Press

is the official series of Southern California's renowned music school, Musicians Institute. **MI** instructors, some of the finest musicians in the world, share their vast knowledge and experience with you – no matter what your current level. For guitar, bass, drums, vocals, and keyboards, **MI Press** offers the finest music curriculum for higher learning through a variety of series:

ESSENTIAL CONCEPTS
Designed from MI core curriculum programs.

MASTER CLASS
Designed from MI elective courses.

PRIVATE LESSONS
Tackle a variety of topics "one-on-one" with MI faculty instructors.

KEYBOARD

Blues Hanon
by Peter Deneff • **Private Lessons**
00695708.............................$14.95

Dictionary of Keyboard Grooves
by Gail Johnson • **Private Lessons**
00695556 Book/CD Pack $16.95

**Funk Keyboards –
The Complete Method**
by Gail Johnson • **Master Class**
00695336 Book/CD Pack $14.95

Jazz Chord Hanon
by Peter Deneff • **Private Lessons**
00695791.............................$12.95

Jazz Hanon
by Peter Deneff • **Private Lessons**
00695554.............................$12.95

Keyboard Technique
by Steve Weingard • **Essential Concepts**
00695365.............................$12.95

Keyboard Voicings
by Kevin King • **Essential Concepts**
00695209.............................$12.95

Music Reading for Keyboard
by Larry Steelman • **Essential Concepts**
00695205.............................$12.95

R&B Soul Keyboards
by Henry J. Brewer • **Private Lessons**
00695327 Book/CD Pack..................$16.95

Rock Hanon
by Peter Deneff • **Private Lessons**
00695784.............................$12.95

Salsa Hanon
by Peter Deneff • **Private Lessons**
00695226.............................$12.95

DRUM

**Afro-Cuban Coordination
for Drumset**
by Maria Martinez • **Private Lessons**
00695328 Book/CD Pack.................$14.95

Blues Drumming
by Ed Roscetti • **Essential Concepts**
00695623 Book/CD Pack.................$14.95

Brazilian Coordination for Drumset
by Maria Martinez • **Master Class**
00695284 Book/CD Pack.................$14.95

**Chart Reading Workbook
for Drummers**
by Bobby Gabriele • **Private Lessons**
00695129 Book/CD Pack.................$14.95

Double Bass Drumming
by Jeff Bowders
00695723 Book/CD Pack.................$19.95

Drummer's Guide to Odd Meters
by Ed Roscetti • **Essential Concepts**
00695349 Book/CD Pack.................$14.95

**Funk & Hip-Hop Grooves
for Drums**
by Ed Roscetti • **Private Lessons**
00695679 Book/CD Pack.................$14.95

Latin Soloing for Drumset
by Phil Maturano • **Private Lessons**
00695287 Book/CD Pack $14.95

**Musician's Guide
to Recording Drums**
by Dallan Beck • **Master Class**
00695755 Book/CD Pack $19.95

**Working the Inner Clock
for Drumset**
by Phil Maturano • **Private Lessons**
00695127 Book/CD Pack $16.95

VOICE

Harmony Vocals
by Mike Campbell & Tracee Lewis • **Private Lessons**
00695262 Book/CD Pack $17.95

**Musician's Guide to
Recording Vocals**
by Dallan Beck • **Private Lessons**
00695626 Book/CD Pack $14.95

Sightsinging
by Mike Campbell • **Essential Concepts**
00695195.............................$17.95

Vocal Technique
by Dena Murray • **Essential Concepts**
00695427 Book/CD Pack.................$22.95

OTHER REFERENCE

Approach to Jazz Improvisation
by Dave Pozzi • **Private Lessons**
00695135 Book/CD Pack.................$17.95

Encyclopedia of Reading Rhythms
by Gary Hess • **Private Lessons**
00695145.............................$19.95

Going Pro
by Kenny Kerner • **Private Lessons**
00695322.............................$17.95

Harmony & Theory
by Keith Wyatt & Carl Schroeder • **Essential Concepts**
00695161.............................$17.95

Home Recording Basics
featuring Dallan Beck
00695655 VHS Video $19.95

Lead Sheet Bible
by Robin Randall and Janice Peterson •
Private Lessons
00695130 Book/CD Pack.................$19.95

FOR MORE INFORMATION, SEE YOUR LOCAL MUSIC DEALER,
OR WRITE TO:

HAL•LEONARD®
CORPORATION
7777 W. BLUEMOUND RD. P.O. BOX 13819 MILWAUKEE, WI 53213

Visit Hal Leonard Online at **www.halleonard.com**

Prices, contents, and availability subject to change without notice

0304